Rais
Jo

MW01120093

The University Professor

Dr Randall J Dyck

Published by Dr Randall J Dyck, 2016.

THE UNIVERSITY PROFESSOR

First edition. April 20, 2016.

Written by Dr Randall J Dyck.

This book is dedicated to all of the amazing students in the world and to those who support their efforts. I have had the privilege of meeting some of you but I wish that I could meet all of you. Your triumphs and struggles often go unacknowledged. You deserve to be taught very well. You are the future of society.

Preface

You cannot open a book without learning something. (Confucius)

This story started out as an autobiography, based on notes from my university teaching career, with flashbacks to my own times as a student, and from my own experiences while working. As the story developed it became more like a novel, with intrigue and some humorous sidelines. A decision was made to turn it into autobiographical fiction, where most of the story is based on facts that occurred over a lifetime, along with some artistic embellishments to connect the flow of scenes as they developed.

The story also contains a helpful discussion guide at the end of it for reading groups, so that they may discuss the ideas that are presented in the story.

At the start of each chapter, some words of wisdom and insight have been added from both Chinese and Western philosophers. My own life and career has been influenced by philosophers such as Lao Tzu, Confucius, Socrates, Plato, and Aristotle.

Even though the story focuses on the challenges, rewards, and setbacks of an instructor and his students at pivotal points during a single term in a university, it has flashbacks from a decade of learning, and from two decades of applying knowledge.

Follow along with the instructor on his journey. The story starts with him conducting a class and then moves on to his activities while preparing to review current material to get his students ready for their future careers. It carries through to his testing experiences and to his preparations for new courses. Every second chapter has flashbacks to those events from his past studies and work where special moments occurred that helped to mold his current character and teaching style.

Along the way, a complete study philosophy emerges.

It is my fervent hope that you enjoy this light hearted look at academic life, and on how education affects all of our lives.

I wish you all the best in your own life and reading pursuits, for both pleasure and for enlightenment.

Chapter 1: The Class

If the teacher is not respected, and the student not cared for, confusion will arise. (Lao Tzu)

Professor Mark Klepin stood gazing at his brightest student with a puzzled look on his face.

'Where in the world did he come up with that question?' he thought.

"Should I repeat the question sir," his student asked.

"No, I heard you. I was just thinking about it."

'How in the world am I going to answer that question in front of the whole class and still make a good impression?' he wondered.

"Actually, that is an excellent question. However, we will not be covering that material until next week. I will have some solutions for you by then," he finally said.

'It will also give me some more time over the next day or two to figure out a good answer for the student,' he thought.

As he looked out over the heads of his students, he tried to envisage what their questions might be during this class. It had been a particularly hard term but the students were now half way through their studies.

The material for this class had a lot of reading and lab assignments to complete. The students also had a group project to work on and their midterm exam would be in a couple of weeks.

He tried to clarify his thoughts before proceeding with the day's lecture.

"OK class. Who can give me an example of how last week's material is currently being used by businesses around the world?"

There was a long pause.

Some of the students looked like they had just woken up. A few were busy typing on their mobile devices. He hoped that they were trying to find examples and not just chatting with their friends. Most of the students actually appeared to be quite interested, but with an expectant look on their faces.

He could recall that last term another instructor had tried to ban all electronic devices from his classroom. One day, he heard a tremendous racket coming from the classroom next door. When he went over to investigate, he saw that one of the students in that room was banging away on a mechanical typewriter. He must have got it from his grandfather. It looked like the entire class was disturbed from the clicking of the typing and from the ringing of the bell at the end of each line. The other instructor soon got the hint and promptly allowed electronic devices back into his classroom again.

One student in Mark's current class timidly raised her hand. "Yes, Marcia?" he asked.

"I don't know the answer but I'm sure that you can give us a much better story than anything that we could come up with. After all, you worked for a really long time before coming here. You must have lots of good stories to share with us."

Mark just rolled his eyes. A number of the other students started nodding their heads in agreement.

After the briefest of pauses, he launched into giving an elaborate solution from a popular company that did business in several countries. He was fortunate that he had worked for a number of years before grinding his way through a doctorate degree. He had thought that teaching would be easier than working. However, he often found that he had to come up with solutions on the spot, such as was happening now.

Marcia looked satisfied but there was still a hungry look in her eyes. Mark wondered about that. The other students began sitting up straighter and leaning forward in their chairs.

"As you can see, even though the material in this course is difficult, it can help you to get better careers after you graduate. Now let's discuss some new material and then see how it can also be used to help you."

"Will you just be covering what is written in the required reading from the textbook, or will you be giving us some more current material that'll help to explain it?" asked Tim. He was one of the students who were struggling with the course. His other instructors had said that he was doing well in their courses. Mark was not sure why he was having such a difficult time with this course.

"Today I will just summarize the important points from the reading material. Next week we will have a full review of everything that has been covered so far so that you and your classmates can get 100 % on the upcoming midterm exam."

There were some snickers from the class.

"Really?"

"Well, maybe not 100 %. However, I do expect everyone to perform much better on the midterm exam than you have done on the quizzes so far. There is still the group project to start thinking about and a comprehensive final exam. You may not feel like it now, but all of the students in the previous terms have always done extremely well in this course by the end of it. Everything will click by then."

"That is a relief, sir. I was starting to think that I was just slow or something."

"Don't worry. Now let's proceed with today's topic," said Mark.

'Now I'll worry about how I'm going to make it seem easy to these students,' he thought.

He began by listing the key points on the board. He then drew some diagrams that explained how the material was to be used in businesses.

Students started asking for more concrete explanations.

"How could we present this information on a website using what you've showed us?"

"And how would we receive customer orders and then update the inventory systems in a business?"

"How would the accounting systems be affected?"

Rather than just show points on the board, Mark activated the computer at the front of the class and illustrated how various software tools could be used to apply the concepts.

"Will we get to use our computers during the midterm and final exams?" a student asked.

"Unfortunately the exam rooms do not come with computers on the desks. I am just giving examples on them so that the concepts are clearer. The exams will only test your basic understanding of the material."

"How about if I bring in my own computer to the exam?" the same student asked.

Mark just smiled.

"Nice try. However, these are closed book exams. You cannot expect to always search for answers on a computer throughout your life. You are expected to have acquired some basic skills from this course and from your other courses as well."

Groans could be heard throughout the classroom.

"I tell you what. How would you feel if I allowed you to bring in some handwritten notes on a single piece of paper as a cheat sheet?"

Cheers erupted in the class.

"Does that mean that I can type up all of my notes and then print them out using a really small font, so that they can all fit on the paper?"

"Again: nice try. Only handwritten notes will be allowed. That way, you will have to think about what are the most important topics that you want to put on your paper, and then you will still have to remember most of the basic concepts. I am not testing to see if you are parrots. I already know that you can copy and paste. I am testing to see if you can think through problems and solve them."

"I guess that I can live with that."

Several students were smiling now. A few still had frowns on their faces.

"However, you can use different colors for your writing if you want to pack in as much information as possible onto your cheat sheets."

"Great idea!" exclaimed one student.

"You can even bring in those magnifying glasses that I see old people using."

There were chuckles among the students now.

Mark continued with the lecture. The mood in the classroom was much lighter than before.

The students realized now that they could just focus on the purpose of the various concepts, and how those concepts were to be used, rather than trying to remember all of the details associated with them.

Mark tried to use a mix of techniques when he had to explain complex material. Key points were written down and then expanded on with notes that he had made from the textbook. The computer was used to show how to apply the material. Questions were then asked of the class, in order to get their opinions on the material.

Mark also gave out basic problems for the class to work on, and then he wandered among the students to monitor their progress to help them out. Finally, he would review the problems a few minutes later to show the students some possible solutions that they could have used.

As he checked on how the students were doing this time, he noticed that Marcia was just staring at her computer screen. "Marcia, do you need me to clarify the question for you?"

"No thanks, Professor. I was just thinking about the different ways that your question could be solved."

'This is an easy problem. What could she be thinking about so deeply?' he wondered.

One student had his hand up so he walked over to see what the student was working on. It turned out that an incorrect setting on the computer had caused it to lose the connection to the network. The student was no longer able to reference the class notes. It was an easy problem to fix, but Mark thought, *'I'd better let the university know so that they can check up on all of the settings for my class.'*

The rest of the students seemed to be doing well. He gave them a few more minutes and then he handed out some more problems for them to consider.

While he was doing that, the fire alarm started ringing with a deafening din. Everyone looked up in panic.

"It is probably just a drill. Follow me outside." Several students could be seen scrambling to repack their backpacks before joining him at the main door.

"I don't think that it's a drill, Professor. Look at all of the fire trucks that are arriving."

Mark debated whether he should rush back in to get his own belongings. However, after a few minutes of hurried activity, it was announced that it was a false alarm and that everyone could return to their classrooms.

Just as everyone was getting reseated in the classroom, the lights went out. There must have been some problem with the building's wiring after all! Mark found that it was quite romantic in the lecture room now, with the only light coming in from the skylight, and from the windows on the doors. Marcia seemed to be staring at him.

"Well...This is interesting! Let's head back outside. I still want to go over a few more of the key concepts with you. It is a sunny day and so I will just lecture on the grass outside. Find a place near the south entrance where you can sit down. I will join you shortly."

The students had never heard of such a thing before, but they were curious to see how the situation developed.

Mark headed over to the supply room to pick up some flipchart paper and a stand. When he went outside he saw that the students were seated in a semi-circle on the grass around a small bubbling fountain. The fragrant smell of fresh cut grass and the sounds of chirping birds greeted his senses.

He set up his stand beside the fountain and proceeded with his lecture as if this was something that he did every day. The students were enthralled, and the other instructors gave him curious glances as they walked by.

The next day, Mark received requests from his other classes that they also wanted to be taught outdoors. In the weeks to come he could frequently be seen outside giving lectures to his students.

The first question that he wrote down on his flipchart stand for today concerned courier companies.

"Think about how you could improve the scheduling of package deliveries."

He gave the students a few minutes and he could see them getting into groups to discuss it with their friends. He then asked them for their ideas, and summarized them on the flipchart paper. He could see that some of them had come up with innovative solutions that he had not considered himself.

The class discussions were off to a good start.

Next he asked them, "Now think about what kind of patterns that you can find in sales data, in order to improve the effectiveness of marketing."

Again, some rather interesting observations were made by his students.

Finally, he asked, "How do the airlines get information to determine the new routes that they want to offer?"

That took them a little longer to consider. They needed to review their notes on ways to interface systems, on government regulations, and on ways to obtain information on the markets, on the economy, and on competitors.

By the end of the class, everyone was discussing the material among themselves and some were even making up their own examples to show to their friends. Mark could not have been more proud of them.

"Are there any final questions on the topics that we have covered today?"

"Can we get some help after class with these topics?" Marcia asked.

"You most certainly may. My office hours are posted outside of the faculty area. You can drop by anytime. Hopefully, the lights will be on by then."

"Thanks. I'll be sure to do that Professor Klepin."

Mark wondered if Marcia had something else on her mind since she was one of the better students in his course. *'Maybe she just wants some advice on jobs that she can apply for?'* he thought.

"Everyone needs to think about the questions that they would like to ask next week. I will be reviewing all of the material. It will be your last chance to clarify it before the exam. You can also send me your questions in advance so that I can focus on them during the review."

"Thanks, Professor."

"Great lecture, sir."

"Have a good weekend, sir."

As the students went back into the building to locate their other classrooms, Mark reflected on their change in attitudes and on how the students were now becoming truly interested in his course.

He had been worried before that this term would be different from previous terms. A number of the students had been struggling over the past few weeks. Now they seemed to have joined the others in their eagerness for the topics.

'*Maybe the university should have a required prep course that teaches new students how to do time management, how to organize notes for learning, how to handle exams, and how to efficiently use the library and computer resources in the university?*' he pondered.

He had seen prep courses used at other universities. They were normally from two to four weeks long and all of the students were required to attend them, and to pass them, before they were allowed to proceed with their full time studies.

The prep courses would usually start by getting the students familiar with the library. They would learn where its various sections were located, its numbering system, and how to use its cataloging systems to locate relevant books. They would also learn how to find peer-reviewed articles for quotes in papers that they would be writing. This would be followed by tutorials on writing formats and on how papers were expected to be organized.

The students would then be shown how to organize the notes that they had taken in class around the subject areas in a course. They would be shown studies that emphasized the importance of taking notes themselves and then practicing what they were learning. This would allow them to more easily grasp the concepts in a course so that they could do well in its exams.

They would be given sample exams so that they could learn the importance of planning the time that they spent on each question based on its points. They would also learn of the details that would be needed in the answers to confirm their mastery of the topics. Marking guidelines for assignments and for exams would be pointed out to them.

The number of study hours that they should expect to spend after classes to get higher grades would be recommended to them. By the end of the prep course, the students learned to appreciate the value of their time and to choose wisely between their study time and their personal time.

Since it was lunch time, Mark headed down to the student food area. There was a faculty food area but he rarely used it.

He found that the students often liked to discuss the course material with him outside of the classroom. Some of them just wanted to chat. This led to a more relaxed environment later on in his classes when he was teaching.

The student food area had over two dozen vendors in it. This was another reason that he preferred it to the faculty food area. The faculty area just had tables and chairs where the staff sat to eat their own lunch that they had brought.

Mark spent a while walking through the student area to check out all of the food choices. Several students noticed him while he was doing this. He finally chose some Japanese food that was cooked on a grill in front of him. The chefs liked to put on a floor show by flipping their spatulas and knives while they were cooking. After collecting his meal he sat down to enjoy it.

It was not long before he was surrounded by students who wanted to discuss the latest technologies with him.

He thought back to his own times as a student and to the challenges that he had faced. He realized that there were many more distractions today that competed for a student's time. Many students had to work part time now to help pay for their studies. They also spent more time playing video games or chatting on social media.

However, Mark assumed that all students were motivated like he used to be.

Chapter 2: Past Studies

Learning is like rowing upstream; not to advance is to drop back. (Chinese Proverb)

Mark Klepin grew up in a small town in the middle of the country. It was more of a gathering place for the farmers in the area and it was one hour away from the nearest city. There was often nothing for him to do in the evenings except to study or to visit relatives.

All of his uncles were farmers but his father had been more interested in starting his own farm equipment dealership. He had been told by his father that all of his uncles had initially chipped in some money to help start the business. It had grown over the years in order to provide services to several of the surrounding communities. A car dealership had also been added to the business in its first few years.

Mark had fond memories of exploring the countryside areas around the town, with a faithful dog that he had named Prince. He had been given Prince as a puppy, and he had nurtured him for many years.

Mark took many trips on his bicycle to see the lush forests and farm lands around the town, and his dog happily followed him everywhere. On one trip Prince chased after a skunk that was happily minding its own business. His dog probably thought that it was a funny looking cat. He got a rude awakening when the skunk sprayed him.

Mark had to bring him home and then promptly wash him in a mixture of hydrogen peroxide that had a little baking soda and liquid dish detergent added to it. Then he rinsed him thoroughly with water to remove all of the smells from him. The farmers in the area had found that this was more effective at removing skunk smells, instead of just covering up the smells with tomato juice bathing.

A few days later, Mark's dog chased after another skunk. He screeched to a halt just before reaching it. He immediately ran off in the opposite direction with his tail between his legs. He must have suddenly remembered the dire consequences of trying to catch such an animal, and so he had rapidly changed his mind.

Prince even came with him to the town's red brick schoolhouse each morning. He was always waiting outside for him when the school day finished. If Mark couldn't see him then he would just call his name. Prince would come running from around the corner of the school. Mark suspected that his dog was probably just busy touring around the town having fun whenever he was in school.

An exciting moment occurred for him in his teens when a farmer gave an unexpected presentation at his school for a show and tell day.

"Watch out!" his classmates shouted to him when he entered the school room that day.

Mark froze and his eyes got very big.

There was a large panting leopard looking back at him from only a few feet away. It was the last thing that he would have expected when he had woken up that morning, and then headed off to school. He had no idea where the farmer had gotten the leopard but it turned out to be very friendly. Everyone enjoyed patting it. He hoped that one day he could have his own leopard as well.

He was surrounded by machinery as he grew up, and he watched how his father's business was run with careful planning, but also with significant risk. Some workers were always getting injured each month. There were even a few fires in the business during his teenage years. But his father just took all of the catastrophes in stride, and carried on with his business activities as usual.

Mark was amazed at the amount of paperwork that was required to run a business, and all of the calculations that were required. He wondered how all of the business processes could be automated to make their operations run more smoothly. He was a fan of science fiction novels, and he had read about how intelligent computers could make decisions all by themselves.

'Surely this can be done today?' he wondered.

He was lucky that the town had built up a large library over the years, in order to provide service to all of the nearby communities. The library was situated in a large sandstone building that used to be the town hall, before the town had moved its administration staff into a newer building. Most of Mark's spare time was spent perusing the fully stocked library shelves.

He was fascinated by what he found in the library's encyclopaedias, travel books, geography books, cultural books, and technology books. His eyes began to open to the possibilities that were available beyond the small town that he found himself in.

He never knew what he was looking for but he was constantly amazed by what he was able to find. He made detailed notes of everything that he read.

He even discovered several topics in some of the books that could help out his uncles in their farming. Farms in the area had been run the same way for generations. Mark read that farmers should plant different crops each season in their fields, in order that one type of crop did not use up all of the nutrients in the land. The books also said that the farmers should leave a different field barren each season, so that the land had a chance to recover its nutrients.

Mark further read that some farmers were setting up bee houses throughout their fields, so that the bees could help pollinate the crops to make them grow better. Other books mentioned that the nutrient makeup of the land had to be matched with the type of treatments that were used on it.

He passed on all of his findings to his uncles. In the next year they reported to him that their crop yields had grown significantly. Soon, the entire community was copying the successful techniques of his uncles.

One of his uncles did some research of his own and discovered that raising buffalo was more profitable than raising cows. So he sold all of his cattle and acquired several buffalo. Mark's parents took him over to see the buffalo during the next weekend.

"Look at what all of the buffalo do when they get scared," his uncle said.

He made a loud noise and they all put their tails straight up and faced him. After about a minute, they put their tails down and then they just started wandering around again.

"Just make sure that you don't scare them when their tails are up or they will charge you."

Mark spent the next hour having fun with the buffalo. He would scare them, wait for a couple of minutes, and then scare them again. It was the most fun that he had had in a while. His parents picked him up later so that he could visit some of his other uncles that weekend.

His father expected him to help out with the family business after he eventually graduated from high school. He already had to help out the uncles on their farms on weekends and during the summers. He also got to drive the large harvesting machines on the farms, years before he had learned to drive a car. Even his nieces were operating large machinery.

'*There has to be more that I can do in life than just hanging around here,*' he thought.

During harvesting season, all of the families would gather together, collect their machinery and then head over to a single farm. Then they would spend a few days cooperating to get the crops in. The guys would focus on working in the fields while the ladies would focus on organizing meals for everyone. A few of the ladies also enjoyed using the large machinery that could be found everywhere at this time.

Some of the farmers often brought over the go-karts that they had made for their kids. The go-karts were only powered by lawn mower engines, and so they were not that powerful. But Mark still had a blast, roaring around the fields in them.

Picnic tables would be set up near the fields, and food would be arranged on them. At lunch time, and at supper time, a horn would be blown to call everyone in. The adults would then be seated together at their tables, and the children would have their own tables to sit at. After another few days, the families would then gather all of their machinery and move on to the next farm. In this manner, all of the crops were harvested in a relatively short time.

Between the harvesting, and his work on the farms at other times of the year, it was getting harder all of the time for Mark to pursue his personal interests and studies.

One day he had had enough.

"Father, I want to go to university to study business and computers," he said.

"Nonsense! Put those silly thoughts out of your mind. My business is doing well. I can teach you everything that you need to know."

"But you could've done so much better. Computers are changing all of the time. I'm sure that there are some great ideas for running businesses that the professors share with their students."

"What do they know? They've never worked a day in their lives."

"Some of them have. And I can explore the city while I'm studying there. I'm sure that I'll make lots of contacts that can help your business in the future."

His father sighed. "I tell you what. I don't see the value of a university education and so I'm not prepared to waste money on it. But if you can find your own money for it, then you can go. Then you can come back here and help me out."

This was not working out the way that Mark had planned.

He had no money. Not counting the little bit that he received from his paper route. He had the contract to deliver all of the newspapers in his town. He had to wake up at 6 AM each morning to deliver them. Upon finishing his deliveries, he would often spend an hour reviewing his school subjects before he had to head off to school.

But he did not want to stay in the small town to do what his father did. He had read about what the world had to offer and he wanted to explore it.

His dreams had to be put on hold for a while.

His father began to show him a few details of how his business was run, and then he got him to help out initially in some non-critical areas of the business. As he learned those areas, his responsibilities were further expanded.

But his mind was still on those things that the rest of the world offered.

That year, a computer club had been created in his school. As part of it, the local university sponsored monthly trips into the nearby city, in order to encourage the high school kids to view their facilities and, hopefully, to attend their university later.

The first time that Mark got into the city, he browsed through the science center at the university but his interests were soon diverted elsewhere. He wanted to take side trips around the city to explore it. First, he took a bus trip downtown to their tallest building and bought a ticket to get to the viewing area at the top of it. He wanted to get a better idea of everything that there was to see and where it was located.

He then took another bus over to the airport. He spent hours that first day, studying the different types of aircraft, and observing their takeoffs and landings.

On his next trip, he checked out the zoo. It seemed that there was always something in the city to catch his interest during his trips there. He looked forward to his monthly trips into the city so that he could explore it.

While he was helping out in his father's business, he was told to take the shop class in the high school to learn more about mechanics. The shop had a variety of different machinery in it, and he even managed to make a few tools. Some of this knowledge came in handy much later in his life, when he helped to design computer systems for some manufacturing companies during his career.

The only negative incident from shop class came when he caught the tip of an index finger in one of the grinding machines. It quickly removed all of the skin on his finger tip, right down to the bone. Mark was more in shock than he was in pain. Some of his classmates were fainting around him.

Mark felt like fainting himself.

The school rushed him to the local clinic, so that they could clean the wound and then bandage it up. When the bandages came off, Mark was surprised to see that now he only had nine fingerprints for his ten fingers. The skin on his index finger had grown back completely smooth. It was years later before the faint outlines of his original fingerprint even started to appear again.

One of the classes that he personally signed up for, in the next school term, was typing. He knew that he wanted to work with computer systems at some point, and he figured that typing skills would be very valuable. Some of the other guys in the school teased him about that. They thought that he was only taking the class in order to be in a room with a lot of ladies. It was true that Mark was the only guy in the class, but he had other ideas on his mind at that time.

Two years later, at the start of his final year of high school, a rather large shock came to him. His grandfather had quietly passed away.

"Mark, your grandfather has left something for you," his father said to him later that week.

He wondered what it could possibly be. *'Maybe it's that beat up motorcycle that he keeps in his garage?'* he thought.

His father then handed him a single envelope. *'Must be the registration papers,'* he assumed.

As he opened it, his eyes grew very large and a wide smile appeared on his face. Inside was a check for thousands of dollars! It would not be enough to get him through university but it was enough to get him through the first year. His dream was alive again! He knew that he could figure out something later on, in order to get through the other years.

"What are you going to do with the money, Mark?"

"I'm going to go to the university, as I mentioned before. I'll study all of the latest business and computer techniques. I'll then share them with you so that you can grow your business even more. You'll see that further studies are worthwhile."

His father just shook his head. He honestly thought that Mark would be back after a year at the university when the money ran out. He still wanted to give him his version of a real education, as he taught him about running a business in more detail, and about how to take care of customers.

Mark had a different vision. A door had opened for him. And now he had to figure out how to get more money for his studies, and how to stretch what he had.

First he approached the principal of his school.

"Are there any scholastic awards that I can apply for at this school?"

His principal knew that Mark was a good student but he was not the best student.

"There are awards of several hundred dollars for each class for the best students in them. These are given out by various local businesses. There is also a graduation award of several hundred dollars for the best student in the final year from all of the schools. It is handed out by the local district school board."

"Do you have any other ideas or suggestions?"

"The university does have a scholarship that is given to the best student overall, from all of the school districts. It pays for all of the required tuition fees for courses taken in the first year when a student attends university. But you would have to study really hard to get that."

Mark needed the money. He could only get it by becoming the best student in every class and in the entire school district. Correction, he needed to become the best student in all of the school districts.

Starting the next day, he approached every teacher and he asked them what other material that he could study, in order to better understand the classes. They were happy to oblige and they soon loaded him up with extra course work.

Mark's friends all thought that he was crazy to spend so much extra time in his studies. However, he wanted to get out of the life that he had, and to explore the world.

Over the next few months, his grades skyrocketed and he managed to become the best student in all of his classes.

His father pulled him aside one day, and then commented to him, "Mark, take it easy. I never had to study so hard. Your grades are already quite good."

"But I want to be the best. I need to be the best."

His father was secretly pleased with him but still thought that all of his drive would evaporate in a year, and then they could work together in the family business. Little did he know!

Mark ended up getting awards for five subjects, plus the award for best student in the school district. When he contacted the university, he was also surprised to be awarded a scholarship for his first year of studies.

He now had enough to pay for his first year of attending the university by using the scholarship. He could use his other award money, and his grandfather's money, to pay for the tuition for his second year at the university, and for all of his residential costs.

There were still four months before the university started and he wanted to prepare for his studies there. He visited the nearby university and obtained the outlines for all of the first year courses that he would be taking. He also bought the textbooks for all of them. Then he visited each professor for those courses.

"Excuse me, I'm sorry to bother you. I'm starting my studies in a few months. I was wondering if there are any problems that I can work on over the summer, to help prepare me for your course?" he asked each professor.

"No bother at all. It is rare to encounter a student who is so eager to begin their studies for my course."

Mark had just spent several months of intense studying to bring up his high school marks. He did not want to just take it easy over the summer. So he threw himself into his university studies to review all of the material that he would need to know.

He decided that he would summarize the most important concepts from each course on a single sheet of note paper. That way, he could then put them above the desk in his room so that he could always refresh his mind on the material with just a glance. This worked so well for him, in helping him to understand the material, that he decided that he would use this method for all of his future studies.

There was a surprise waiting for him when he started registering for his first year of courses at the university. He mentioned to the registrar that he expected to do really well, since he had reviewed all of the courses over the summer.

"Did you know that you can write a challenge exam for any course and then proceed immediately to the next year for that subject?" the registrar said.

"There is such a thing? Where do I sign up to try?"

"Which course do you feel that you want to try?"

"All of them," Mark said.

The registrar had never heard of this before. He made some calls to a few professors. They all agreed that Mark could try their exams in the next week.

"You're all set. Even if you pass only one, it'll still save you some time and money."

Mark spent the rest of the week, and the weekend, reviewing all of the course outlines that he had, and the notes that he had made from their textbooks. He also redid as many of the problems from the books that he could, in the limited time that he had.

When Mark wrote the exams in the following week, he passed every single one of them. He was able to proceed immediately to second year at the university.

He was ecstatic!

He could now start his studies with his second year courses. His university scholarship would pay for those studies. His residential costs, and the tuition for his third year courses, could be covered by his high school award money and by his grandfather's money. He only needed funding for the last year of his studies now.

Word got around and he was soon offered positions marking the first year assignments for a number of the professors. The money was not great but every bit of it helped. He applied himself to his studies and to the work that he was doing after his classes at the university.

One of the perks that he received while working for the professors was the permanent assignment of a small office. It was near to the university's computer labs and it was only big enough for a desk and a chair. But it offered a place of quiet solitude where Mark could do both his grading work and his own studies. The professors also gave him a security code to enter the private computer labs for the faculty. He took advantage of those labs in the evenings, when no one was around, to work quietly on his own assignments.

The university had a huge library and Mark was in heaven perusing its numerous book shelves. There was so much to learn that he had to approach his professors again to find out where he should focus his studies.

"What other topics can I study on my own that further expands on this?" he often asked them.

"I can give you a list and some recommended books, but you will have to practice the material as well if you want to really understand it," he heard more than once from them.

His first two years of studies were quite intense. He spent hours practicing what he was learning and perusing books and other resources to discover new technologies and business processes. He was still worried about how he would get enough money to pay for his final year of studies.

As it turned out, one of his father's business friends told him that there was an evening job at a new computer manufacturing company that had just opened up in a nearby city. They were still looking for a computer operator for their large systems that could help them out at night to monitor its activities. The operator would also have to ensure that all of its printed reports were distributed to the relevant executives by the next morning.

This sounded like a good opportunity but Mark first needed to figure out how he could still do his studies at a university. He did some checking and found out that the new company would be located next to a major university in the other city.

He grabbed a copy of his current university records and got ready to drive over to the nearby city in a car that his father had lent to him, in order to make some inquiries.

He had been told about some country roads that were a shortcut way to the other city. He decided to give it a try. About half way there, he got lost. All that he could see around him for miles was rolling hills, flat land, and a few trees. And all of the roads looked the same. Therefore, he took a road at random, and managed to encounter a farmer a few miles later. From his helpful instructions he was able to proceed once more.

Just when the other city could be seen in the distance, he encountered a herd of cows on the trail that he had been directed to take. Beeping the horn did not cause any movement. The cows just looked up at him and then went back to their grazing.

Mark knew from his childhood that you could not push a cow when it did not want to move. He had heard about kids from the farms, who pushed over the cows for fun, but he did not believe it.

Getting out of his car, he spotted a hay bale near a fence. He went over to it, broke it open, and proceeded to spread it around on the other side of the fence. The cows took notice of his activity and they soon wandered over to investigate. As they say, *the grass always looks greener on the other side of the fence.* The trail was now clear, and so he was able to continue on his way.

He finally managed to get to the new university later that afternoon. It still ended up taking him quite a while to find their administration building where the registrar was located. It was a much larger university than the one where he was currently attending classes.

"Excuse me. Can someone tell me if I can transfer credits from my university in the next city, in order to finish my studies at this university?"

"Certainly. We get similar requests all of the time. We would be happy to have you attend our university. Let's look at your academic transcripts, and then we can fill out the required documents."

The other university was able to give him credits for all of his courses, except for one. It would mean that he would have to overload himself with courses in his final year but he was confident that he could do it.

Next he visited the new computer manufacturing company and applied for the job that had been referred to him. The company was impressed with both his knowledge of current technologies and with his academic records.

"Would you also be comfortable in working with bleeding edge technology?"

Mark had visions of working with their manufacturing machines and getting cut to pieces. He had thought that this was just a job for a computer operator.

"Sounds dangerous," he cautiously replied.

"It is perfectly safe. It is for a new technology that we are developing. We are hoping to introduce it to the marketplace next year. We will get you to run tests on some of the new software and computer hardware while you are here in the evening. How does that sound?"

"It sounds a lot better than what I was thinking just now. I'm always excited by new technologies."

"Do you think that you could start working for us this July?"

"I was hoping for something sooner but that's acceptable."

"Can you also continue to help us out, once you start your university studies again?"

"For sure! I really appreciate this opportunity. I'm happy to help you out for as long as you need me."

The company was delighted with his attitude. They signed him up as an employee on the spot. It was his first real job!

He made enough money during the next year to support his last year of studies at the university. It was an intense year, as he had thought. He also had some awkward moments in his first month at the new university finding out where all of his classrooms and his computer labs were. He was only getting a few hours of sleep each night, due to the new job, and a few times he had even nodded off to sleep in class!

But he finally made it. He got his university degree, with majors in both business and in computers. All of his hard work and studies had paid off. He felt that getting a degree was like climbing a mountain. It took a lot of training and a lot of hard work.

At times he reached obstacles and he was not sure if he could continue. However, eventually he reached the top and the view was fantastic. That was when he had realized that all of the hard work was worth it!

He ended up landing a job with a local consulting company that had a few dozen employees. They were impressed by the business knowledge and technical expertise that he had acquired from his university studies. His extra studies and his practices with different technologies had also helped.

He then spent awhile traveling around his country and applying his knowledge. Later, he joined a large international consulting company that had a few hundred employees. They gave him the opportunity to consult in other countries as well.

He saw lots and learned lots over the next few years. Little did he know that there were more studies to come, along with a lot more challenges!

Chapter 3: The Notes

Well begun is half done. (Aristotle)

After arriving home later that day from teaching at the university, Mark was ready to just unwind. His ex-wife had never afforded him that privilege during the years that he had been with her. She had three completely different university degrees (two were studied at the same time back in her country) and she came from a large business family. She considered herself very smart, since her degrees were in electrical engineering, business, and computer science.

"Do you realize how much money you're losing by just sitting there?" he could recall her saying. "You could be out consulting now with your own private company this evening and this coming weekend."

He had fond memories of her but he was happy now that he could just relax and *smell the roses*, as they say.

The first order of business for him was to try to figure out how he was going to answer the question that his bright student had posed to him in the class today. He always liked to review the day in his mind, before moving onto other matters that needed to be addressed.

'I guess that I'll start by seeing if anyone else has a simple example that I can use,' he thought.

He started his search by using his computer to look at what others were discussing. It took him a few tries with different keywords, but he eventually found some material that was relevant. However, it was all too complex for him to show to the students. He was not sure if he would even use it himself, since he had a hard time understanding what he saw. He was sure that there must be a better way to do it.

Next he flipped through his old dusty textbooks and some training manuals that he had kept from his own studies. Some of them were from those times many years ago when he was just starting to do consulting. This time, all of the examples that he saw were more fundamental in nature, since the references were only focused on teaching concepts, and not on showing how to apply the concepts.

'*Hmmm...Let me try a different approach,*' he thought.

Finally, he just did what he should have from the beginning. He used his computer to slowly build up a basic solution into something that could be applied in several situations. Then, after making a few notes to himself of the steps that were involved, he felt that he had something that could be explained clearly to his students in the following week.

Mark realized that he still had to make up some review notes for next week but that could wait until the weekend. As he was walking over to his kitchen to prepare something to eat, his phone rang.

"Hello?"

"Mark, guess who this is?"

He recognized the voice of one of his friends who was teaching at another university. "Hi Cindy. What's up?"

Cindy was quite a bit younger than him and he had met her a year ago at a business conference in the city. He had been giving a presentation at the time on how to take advantage of leading edge techniques, in order to improve overall business operations.

"I'm having some problems using the new software that the university installed. By any chance, can I get some personal help from you?" she replied.

"Not a problem. I was just about to prepare something to eat. Why don't you meet me over at the new shopping mall, and then we can grab some fast food and chat about your concerns?"

"That sounds good. Can you also make some time to drop over to my office tonight at the university? There won't be anyone around, and so you can show me the best way to use my software, without any interruptions."

Mark wondered if there were other reasons for this meeting. Cindy was fairly bright and she could probably figure out everything by herself. However, he wanted to appear helpful.

"Sure. I'll see you over at the mall in a short time. Let's meet in the food court over there."

Grabbing his coat, he headed out the door. He hesitated for a bit wondering which car he should bring. He had an American car that he used for travel to the university, and for his trips around the city. He also had a European car that his consulting revenue had allowed him to buy, before he had become a professor. He normally only used it to attend parties and business conferences, but he decided that it would make a good impression this time.

When he arrived at the mall, he was lucky to get a parking spot that was fairly close to the main door. He knew that it would take Cindy a little while longer to arrive, and so he decided to first visit the computer store in the mall. He always enjoyed exploring the latest technology, and he also wanted to have the same *toys* that his students were using.

"Hi Mark. I haven't seen you for a while," said the store manager, as he greeted him with a firm handshake.

"Sorry, Tony. I've been quite busy this term at the university. So what's new?"

"We have lots of new things but you really need to upgrade your phone first if you want to interface to them. Your phone is outdated now and not cool."

"Really? That fast? I just got it a short time ago."

"Technology changes quickly. Here, let me show you some things that will interest you."

Tony spent the next few minutes pointing out some really neat items to Mark.

It was overwhelming!

Mark was finding it harder every year to keep up with all of the latest technological changes. He already had to modify his course outlines every term to include new technologies. He often had to spend his summers exploring them, just so that he could present current illustrations to his students on the best way to take advantage of them.

Time was running short and so Mark thanked Tony, and then he headed over to the food court to wait for Cindy.

She was arriving just as he got there, so his timing turned out to be impeccable. Cindy looked ravishing. Her dressing was always first rate, unlike his more casual dressing in the evenings.

"So Mark, what do you want to eat? They have lots of choices at this mall. There is Japanese, Chinese, Italian, Mexican, Greek, and of course lots of American food outlets."

"As long as my food doesn't walk or crawl off my plate, I'm good with it," he replied.

She laughed. "OK, let's try Italian today. We can sit at that table in the corner near the restaurant."

As they collected their food orders and walked towards their table, Mark wondered how detailed her questions were going to be. The software that her university used was quite different from that used by his university. He continued to ponder this for the next few minutes while they ate in silence.

"Mark, you look puzzled."

"I'm just trying to figure out how I can help you with your new software."

"My software is fine. I just needed some pointers on how to integrate it into my classes now. You seem to do that so well with new technologies."

"I might make it look easy but there is a lot of work that I do behind the scenes," he said.

"And I want to lean on your expertise. I think that there is a lot that you could teach me," she winked at him.

"I appreciate your confidence in my abilities. Perhaps this is a good time to go over to your office to take a look at your software?"

"That would be wonderful. Do you mind if we wander around the shopping mall first for a few minutes? I want to check out all of the sales that the stores are putting on this week."

Their few minutes of wandering stretched out to a couple of hours. It was quite late by the time that they were ready to go to their cars and then to head over to her university.

"Where did you park your car Mark?"

"There it is. It's the silver one by the door."

"Wow! Your university must pay its professors quite a bit more than what my university pays its faculty."

"Not at all. I bought it years ago with the revenue that I made from consulting before I joined the university. Those times were a completely different life and a lot more stressful."

"I would be very interested in hearing some more details about it at a later time. For starters, let's just head over to my office and then you can take a look at my software."

"That would be fine. It's getting late and I still want to get a good rest tonight. I have a class tomorrow that I need to get ready for, and I still want to make up some review notes for my students over the weekend."

Cindy gave him a sideways glance and just smiled.

Mark followed Cindy over to her university. He had some trepidation and wondered if he could satisfy what she needed. He did have experience with many types of software and integrating it into business systems and also into academic ones. However, Cindy seemed to be a lot more focused on software than he was. *'Maybe her interpretation of it is different?'* he thought.

Upon arriving at the university they both had to sign in first at the security desk, since it was after the regular class times.

"Are the two of you going to be very long?" asked the security guard.

"Depends on how quickly my fellow professor can help me out," replied Cindy.

"Don't stay too late. The university is shutting down all of their systems at midnight for backups and another major upgrade to their software."

"Unbelievable! I think that I'll need some more of your time in the near future Mark," said Cindy, as she turned to look at Mark.

He hesitated for just a moment. "Of course, Cindy. Feel free to call me up anytime to help you out with your systems."

Cindy had a satisfied look on her face as she led Mark down a passageway to the elevator. They took it up to the floor that her office was on. It was quiet at that time of the night and Cindy had an office that looked out over the peaceful university grounds. Her office was small but the view made it seem bigger than it was.

"Sit beside me Mark while I call up the new systems and show you what they can do. Then you can give me some ideas about how I can use them in my classrooms."

"Show me what you're doing that's causing you problems."

"Now you remind me of the computer expert in the joke about three persons traveling down a steep mountain road," Cindy laughed, while covering her mouth.

"I didn't hear that one. How does it go?"

"There is a computer expert, an engineer, and a priest in a car going down a steep road. Suddenly the brakes fail. After much panic and stressful driving they barely manage to make it to the bottom of a mountainous hill. Once they get the car stopped then they all step out of it with their hearts beating rapidly. The priest gives thanks for making it down the hill safely. The engineer suggests that they pull the car apart to see what the problem is. The computer expert says that they should drive the car back up to the top of the hill to see if the problem repeats itself."

"Ha! Am I really like that? I just need to understand your problems in more detail so that I can suggest the best solutions for you," he responded defensively.

"Just relax Mark. I know that you're only trying to help. Now please take a look at my software."

The two of them had to sit close together in her narrow office so that he could examine her software and he found it hard to concentrate at first. He did try to make suggestions to her as the night wore on and he ended up showing her how to do quite a few things that night. They did not manage to finish until two hours later and then they finally said their goodbyes.

As he drove home, Mark reflected on his time with Cindy. He would be pleased to be able to spend more time with her. She had similar interests to his own right now but he would like to know more about her life before the university.

He was sure that everyone had quite a different upbringing than his own. His was not a typical childhood and he was not a typical student when he was at university. He had had a limited social life due to the studying that he had to do to ensure that he could finish his university degree and then get a good job afterwards.

He had married right after university, and his wife at that time had been introduced to him by fellow students. She had immigrated to his country to study and work.

Mark never did develop a lot of skills for dating and socializing.

His work life had been quite stressful back then, with lots of traveling and deadlines for major projects. Even when he came home his wife used to strongly encourage him to do some consulting on the side, in order to earn extra income and to build up a large client list for future business opportunities. As a result, he rarely ended up socializing with others.

Even now, he often spent his free time researching new technologies and business processes to improve the content of his university courses. Good for the students, not so good for him.

When he made it home, and was in the process of waiting for his garage door to open, a young deer wandered around the corner of his house and bolted into his now open garage. He lived near a park and the deer often came over to visit. He thought about closing his garage door again to catch the deer for a pet, but he ended up simply getting out of his car and saying, "Shoo!"

Finally arriving inside his home, he just crashed on his sofa. He was so worn out that he did not have the energy to walk upstairs to his bedroom.

The next morning, he awoke with a fresh outlook on life. He realized that he had to create a balance between his work life at the university and his personal life.

'All right then. Let me see if I can distill my experiences down into something useful that I can pass on to my students,' he thought.

'I was taught a lot of material during my undergraduate, graduate, and doctoral studies at various universities. When I started working, I realized that some of it wouldn't help me at all in my career, and the material that would help me wasn't explained clearly in the classes that I took.'

He wanted his students to have solid skills that they could rely on when they graduated. He needed to determine what he could get the students to focus on, and he wanted to make sure that he taught mainly those skills in his review with them the next week.

The university had a lot of theoretical material that had to be taught but the application of that material in the business world for different situations was rarely taught by others.

Mark wanted to point out to the students what material they should focus on, and then he had to reinforce this with real life examples that the students could work on.

His hope was that they would then have more time for a decent social life because he could eliminate the extra studying time that they would have to spend in understanding concepts. He could also give them more social time later on as they started work, since they wouldn't need to take extra courses like he did, or to spend long hours at work trying to figure out material that was not taught in enough detail at the university.

Throughout the next day as he was conducting his classes, he thought about how he could improve his courses even further. Some of his students even commented to him that he seemed to be preoccupied that day with other thoughts.

That weekend he began reviewing his notes from the current term. He isolated the key parts that would be useful for the students later in their careers, and then he made up some examples that he could share with the class.

'*This is a much better approach than the way that I was taught,*' he reflected.

Over the rest of the weekend he kept thinking back to his own work time, the issues that he had encountered, and which parts of his studies were the most useful for businesses. As he did this, he built up a new set of notes that he could use in his classroom the next week.

He was sure that the students would be ecstatic, and that their eyes would open to the possibilities that the knowledge in his course could give to them.

Chapter 4: Past Memories

Constant knowledge is called wisdom. (Lao Tzu)

Mark began his career with a small local consulting company of a few dozen employees in the city where he graduated. He figured that he was fortunate to have joined them, instead of a larger firm like many of the other graduates did. The pay was lower but the company allowed him to work in different areas so that he could improve his skill sets, and so that he could see how their different clients ran their business operations.

Many of his friends worked in a single company, in a single department, and were assigned specific tasks that used only a small portion of their university skills. They never got to work with executives or others from outside their department.

Mark was routinely required to work with the executives and the staff in all of the departments at various businesses, as he helped them to solve their problems. He found out that the knowledge that he had gained from growing up in his father's business was very useful to him after all.

Travel was another benefit that he enjoyed. He was often asked to visit business clients in other cities to analyze their needs. While he was there, he got some time to tour around the cities and their communities, after each of his work days had concluded. This gave him a broad exposure to different cultures and ways of thinking. As well as many styles of food. He enjoyed them all. He would eat anything that walked, swam, or flew. He drew the line at anything that slithered or crawled. The more spicy the food, the better he liked it.

He often wandered the historic parts of cities to admire their different architectural styles. Some of his clients took him out to scenic golf courses or out on sailboats when lakes were nearby. He also saw a number of glorious waterfalls, and some of the cities were near mountains where he could take in some skiing at their wonderful resorts.

One of his more memorable business trips was when he got to see a rodeo in one of those cities. The rodeo simulated the lifestyle of cowboys and the fun that they had. There were a number of events that they had to compete in. One of them was to catch a runaway cow. They would chase it with a horse, and either accurately throw a rope around its neck, or jump off of their horse to wrestle it to a stop.

"Yahoo!" they would shout, upon raising their arms in a victory salute.

They also demonstrated their sense of balance by attempting to ride a bucking bull, or a bucking horse. Points were awarded to them for their riding style. There was a minimum amount of time that they had to stay mounted, in order to get the full credit for their ride.

Mark's client in that city was a law firm that was located in a historic building that had lots of stonework and woodwork on it and within it. Mark thought that it looked like a castle. Some people told him that it was haunted but he did not believe them.

While he was working alone later that night, in order to make some urgent changes for the client, he heard the door open in the outer office area. He assumed that it was one of the law partners coming over to check up on him. He heard footsteps approaching him, and then he felt someone behind him. When he turned around, no one was there! The hairs on his neck and arms stood straight up.

'*Maybe this building is haunted,*' he thought.

'*Maybe it's a lawyer ghost,*' he feared.

'*Maybe it's just a friendly cowboy ghost,*' he hoped.

Just to play it safe, he said, "I'm sorry that I'm here so late. My client wants all of these changes finished by tonight. I'm so sorry to disturb you. I'll leave as soon as I can."

Then, to his amazement, he heard the floor creak and then the footsteps moved back towards the main office door. Then he swore that he heard the door open and close again. He went back to the work that he was doing, and endeavored to finish it as quickly as he could. In the morning, no one would believe his story. He figured that the client was just playing some kind of a joke on him, in order to make him work faster, so that his consulting bill would be lower. But he could never be sure.

There was also one time when he received an urgent call from another remote client, shortly after he had returned from this consulting trip. The client was a large manufacturer that produced thousands of different products. They wanted him in their city immediately to help resolve some issues with their business operations. They said that their president was in his city on business, and that he would be coming back in a couple of hours.

They asked him, "Would you mind riding back with him on the corporate jet?"

Mark couldn't wait to get to the airport to join the president. He felt like a billionaire on that trip! It was like having a private jet for himself. While the president made calls and did other work, Mark chatted with the pilots and watched how they operated the plane.

When they landed, the president was greeted at the airport by a chauffeur who was driving a stretched limousine. Mark got to ride in style with the president over to the corporate office. He solved the problems at the client site in short order, but then he had to take a taxi back to the airport and a basic commercial flight back home.

Another time, a local courier client that operated a few dozen vehicles called him up in a panic. Mark grew increasingly alarmed as the owner explained the situation.

"You did what?" he exclaimed.

It turned out that one of the client's executives had accidentally deleted the security account on their system. Now they had no way to set up new users, or to do administrative work on their system. Mark grabbed his coat and headed over to the client's site to see what he could do.

He needed security access to the client's system but a normal user account would not allow him to resolve the problem. After some thought, he realized that there was a way to re-activate the security account, if it would work. He had never tried this before.

He located a program on the client's system that was originally built using the security account. It was a yearend program that was used to clean up the system. He needed to replace the command inside it with one that created a new security account. The problem was that if he simply rebuilt the program then it would be running under normal user authority. It would ignore the command that he put inside it.

So he found the actual location of the yearend program on the client's disk drives. Then he used a disk repair program to replace its command by a create command for a security account. When he ran the yearend program, it executed his command instead of the one that it had originally been built to run. The alternative would have been to reinstall the client's entire system, along with all of the data from their backups.

The client was ecstatic and more work soon followed from them.

Since Mark was just starting out in his career and there was so much travel involved, he and his wife Evelyn just rented apartments for a while. She had recently immigrated to his country and so she only worked part time, or on contracts. Due to this, she was able to accompany him on many of his business trips.

He never did get around to having a formal vacation with her, since she was always pushing him to work through his holidays, his weekends, and his evenings. Her thinking was that it was better to earn money while there was high demand and then to enjoy it later. Maybe that was correct, but it was a hard life on him for the first few years that he was working.

One day he asked his wife, "Why don't we just stop eating and sleeping? We could earn a fortune consulting during meal times and during the night."

"Ha! Don't be silly. Everyone has to eat and sleep."

"Look at what other families are doing. Don't you think that we also need to come home and relax in the evening, and then visit our friends on the weekends?"

"They are all just lazy. My parents worked every minute to build up their business. They never needed to relax or socialize."

"I can see that they are still working. They are too ill to travel now and to enjoy life. There must be a limit to how long that people should work."

"They can retire when they are 80. We can retire when we are 80."

"I think that work life, study life, and personal life should have a balance. I had no social life while I was studying to get into university and then through it. But I didn't intend to spend my entire life like that!"

His wife did not agree and that was the beginning of their drifting apart. He rarely saw her after that as her work increased and her problem solving skills became in demand around the world. That was good for her but not so good for him.

Mark knew that he had to work hard to build up his career. But he also needed his time free in the evening in order to pursue advanced studies, so that he would not always be doing the same job for the rest of his life.

And he also wanted some time on the weekends to explore new technologies so that his skills would not become outdated. It was not just socializing, or being lazy, as his wife thought. Well, maybe a little of that.

After his conversation, he began to plan out a new life in order to secure his future. He immediately took weekends off so that he could investigate new technologies, or to just relax with short trips to a lake so that he could get rid of his stress.

He was worried that he would pass away from a heart attack if he kept working the way that he was, or get an ulcer or appendix attack. His wife continued to do her own weekend and evening work and she did not see the point of all of these activities.

Mark also dropped all of his evening work at that time, and then he began to take a number of courses to improve his business and computer skills. In addition to this he checked out the times when business and technology conferences were being conducted. He arranged to attend them so that he could build up his knowledge of current topics.

While he was attending one of these conferences at a large coastal city, he was approached by a client that recognized him.

"Mark, what brings you to our fair city?"

"This conference looked like a useful place to pick up some ideas for using new technologies."

"Based on the way that you improved our business operations, I think that you should be conducting the seminars at this conference, and not just attending them."

"Thank you for your vote of confidence. I just apply some common sense and what I have learned, in order to design systems that work."

"It is more than that. You grew up in a business. You know how we think. You are comfortable around technology."

Mark blushed. He wasn't used to such high praise.

"I tell you what. I know the conference coordinator. Let's go talk to him and see if he'd be interested in getting you to give one of the seminars at the end of this year."

Mark followed Brad, his client, over to one of the offices that were at the side of the conference hall.

"Steve, this is Mark. He has done some consulting work for us over the last few years. I think that you should take advantage of his business and technological skills to present to your members."

"Hi Mark. Pleased to meet you. What are you working on now that you could share with us?"

"Well…I just started looking at integrating the systems in one of our business clients to the banking networks for credit authorizations and reconciliations. I won't be finished that for a few months."

"Could you make up a presentation for it by the end of this year? I am sure that our members would love to hear about it. We would even be willing to pay for your trip down here, along with your housing costs, to help pay for your time. We will also cover all of your conference fees so that you can attend any event while you are here."

"When you put it that way, how can I refuse? I will stay in touch with you over the next few months as I implement the system for the client."

"Perfect. We will see you at the end of the year."

That was the start of Mark's public speaking. He went on to speak at other events, at company training sessions, and at some evening courses in a local college as a guest lecturer. He loved it!

He was approached by an international consulting company a couple of years after he had started taking these extra evening classes and doing his public speaking. He was offered a position building systems for their clients. He found that his time working with new technologies on the weekends had helped to prepare him for this new job and so he took it.

He would not have had this opportunity, had he continued working every minute of every day, had he not taken extra courses, had he not explored new technologies, or had he skipped conferences.

At that moment, he vowed to continue his studies and to continue investigating new business and computer processes.

His new job allowed him to visit businesses in other countries. His knowledge of cultures and business practices grew at a phenomenal rate. Within a short time, he had visited over a dozen countries. Most of them were in the Far East.

He even had to get a new passport a couple of times, due to all of the visitation and visa stamps on the pages inside of it.

There was one year that he was sent to a large computer conference in Singapore to learn about the latest technologies. While the conference proved to be interesting, the night markets in Singapore proved to be even more interesting to him. They were always buzzing with activity and numerous vendors. Not to mention the tantalizing smells of spicy meats sizzling over outdoor cooking grills.

In all of the Asian cities that he had visited there were always a variety of night markets for food, and for products of all kinds. He often had to get local business associates to help him with haggling for the best price in those markets. He was even able to obtain technologies at that time that did not show up in western markets until years later.

While at the computer conference, he noticed an office building in Singapore that had a rather large square hole right in the middle of it. He asked one of the local residents, "Why is there a hole in the middle of that building over there?"

"That is so that our dragon can come down to the sea to drink and bathe."

"What?"

"We believe in feng shui. It concerns the placement of buildings in relation to their environment and the placement of items within them. That building would have blocked our local dragon, and so the architects put an opening in it that was more auspicious. Otherwise, every business in it and around it would have suffered bad luck."

"Seriously?"

"It is better to be safe than sorry. Our traditions and beliefs go back thousands of years. Every one of our architects, engineers, and real estate agents must take a course on feng shui. The business people and the workers are all aware of it, and so the professionals must also take it into account."

"I have never seen a dragon. What time does he come through the city?"

"It's only his spirit that comes through our city and so you won't be able to see him. Or so they teach us."

Mark couldn't help but wonder if there were dragon spirits flying around in his own country. It was another item to add to his list of items to consider when he was consulting with businesses.

He had become quite interested in all managerial challenges from his various business trips, and in the integration of all business processes. MBA's were a hot topic and many executives held them. Mark felt that a Master's in Business Administration could enhance his career significantly at this point.

But how could he get it? He did not want to just give up his career and go back to school for a couple of years. It would take him forever to get started again. He decided to approach the president of the consulting company that he worked for to ask for his advice.

"Bob, I think that our clients would value our services more highly if I also had an MBA behind my name. But I don't want to leave you stranded by just up and leaving for a couple of years. Do you have any thoughts on this matter?"

"Didn't you know that you can now study for an MBA on evenings and on weekends? They call them accelerated programs. They are intended for those individuals that have existing business experience. That would be perfect for you. Do you want me to make some calls for you? I know a number of the deans that oversee these programs."

Mark was elated! "That is very kind of you. I would really appreciate it."

By the next week, Bob had obtained information from all of the business schools in the area so that he could discuss them with Mark. Most of the schools had a mix of evening and weekend studies. Most of them required that two or three weeks a year be spent at their campuses. However, one of the schools had a program that could be done strictly with evening studies, and it had no requirement that time be taken away from work.

Some of the schools had MBA programs that were thesis based but a number of the others were course based. Those that were only course based had more material to study but students would be able to get through them in a couple of years. The thesis based MBA programs started with a few fundamental courses on advanced business processes. But then students had to use that knowledge to solve an actual business problem. Depending on whether they encountered difficulties in their solutions, and on whether their university committee accepted their solution, the students in thesis based programs could spend a few more years before everything was acceptable.

The business school that Bob had found that taught classes only in the evening was course based.

"This looks good Bob but will a degree from that school mean anything? I may want to do doctoral studies for a PhD later on, and I don't want to close any doors."

"Look at this report about the school, Mark. They are listed as one of the 100 best graduate schools in the world, and their prices are quite reasonable compared to the other schools. Plus it is course based and so you can finish it within two years."

"Looks good! I guess I know what I will be doing for the next two years after I get home from work each day."

Mark couldn't wait to tell the news to his wife that night.

"Evelyn, I'm going to study for an MBA!"

"What do you want to do that for? I don't have one. My parents don't have one. You don't have to have an MBA to be successful."

"But it opens up new possibilities. Think of all of the opportunities that will be available."

"You already make enough money and have a good job. I suggest that you just spend the time doing more private consulting, instead of spending more time studying."

Mark couldn't agree with his wife's viewpoint and he felt that an MBA would make their lives better in the long run. However, she strongly disagreed with him and she continued to drift apart from him over the next two years of his studies.

Between his day job consulting and traveling, and his night time studies, Mark felt like he was busy 24 hours a day for 7 days a week. It was a very challenging time for him during the studies for his master's degree.

In the first course that he took, he got an X! He was expecting an A but this looked really bad. He was sure that he knew the material inside out. He knew about grades of A, B, C, and D. These could be further designated with a plus or minus sign. He also knew about grades of F, for failing a course, I, for incomplete work, which was given when a university was waiting on some final assignments, and W, for a withdrawal from a course.

He had previously seen a grade of E, when he had been granted exemptions from courses in his undergraduate years. In later years, he would also learn about the grade of N, which was given for non-credit, or audit, status in courses taken by special students.

But a grade of X boggled his mind. At least it wasn't a Z!

In trepidation, he called up the university's administration office to inquire on his grade.

"Hi. I just received a grade of X on my latest course. I don't understand what that grade means. Can you please explain it to me?"

"We are sorry about your confusion. We always get inquiries about our X grades. They stand for exceptional work. We rarely give them out to students. They are above an A grade."

"You cannot imagine how relieved that makes me feel. Thank you for your time."

In the ensuing years of his MBA studies, Mark managed to obtain quite a few of these X grades.

By the time that he had his MBA, his wife had already divorced him to do consulting contracts around the world. He slowly lost contact with her over the years but the last time that he heard, she was still working days, evenings, and weekends to maximize her earnings.

He found that his consulting work did increase once he got his MBA. It seemed to be easier to get contracts, the contracts paid better, and the work was more challenging.

He had also acquired an interest in the academic world while he was pursuing his advanced studies.

He approached one of the local universities that had a few thousand students and asked their administrators if he could teach an evening course for them. He was surprised when they readily accepted. They said that he could start in a couple of months. So he spent extra time during the next few weeks, after his work, preparing material for the course that he would be teaching.

He would be teaching a course on designing systems. He realized from his work experience that there was a lot that the students would have to be made aware of. He began by gathering a number of materials and then making some notes from them.

He started by summarizing development methods, time estimating formulas, project control milestones, audit controls, and quality assurance planning. To these, he added notes on data structures, interface formats, performance analysis, security configurations, and diagramming tools. By the end of the summer, he felt that he was ready for the university.

That September, he taught his course on designing systems. It lasted for four months and at the end of it, the university offered him a full time contract to teach several more courses over the next few years. The money was less than he had been making but he found that he really enjoyed teaching, plus the university offered to pay for his doctoral studies as well.

Mark wondered how he would fit into this new lifestyle and if he had made the right choice.

Chapter 5: The Review

Employ your time in improving yourself by other's writings, so that you shall gain easily what others have labored hard for. (Socrates)

"Good morning, everyone," Mark greeted his students.

"Good morning, sir."

"As I said last week, we are only reviewing material this week in order to prepare you for the midterm exam next week. I have received a few messages on topics that you would like me to focus on. But first, I will point out an easy solution to the problem that was raised last week."

"It might be easy for you, professor, but this is the first time that we're seeing a lot of this material," said Tim, as he looked around at the rest of the class.

"I think that you will find that my example today and the review notes that I will cover with you will make all of the material for this term crystal clear. I spent a lot of time over the weekend picking out the material that will be most useful to your careers when you graduate."

There was applause from some of the students in the room. Several hands went up.

"You mean we don't have to know every little detail in the course?"

"That sounds cool. Why don't all of the professors do that?"

"How do you know what's used by businesses?"

"Will the rest of the course be easier now?"

Mark could see that he had opened up a door that could not be closed now. He reflected on the best way that he could explain everything to his students.

"This course is based on current research about business practices and on the technologies that businesses use to become more competitive in the marketplace. Therefore, it has a lot of concepts and techniques in it that a few of you might have been struggling with.

"There are a few key methods that you must understand. All of the other techniques are based on them. You can always review the details later when you are working and need them.

"Also, I am able to identify the key methods due to my years of consulting for various businesses, and due to the contacts that I maintain with many of those businesses. Some of your courses here at the university are based more on theories to introduce concepts, and so you would be tested on all of the theories that they discussed."

"I think that I know which courses you are thinking about," one student said. There was some nodding and glances in the classroom as the other students agreed.

"Does that mean that you can find jobs for all of us after we graduate?"

"I have already passed on the names of the businesses that I have worked with to the university's career office. They can help you with finding businesses to apply to," Mark said.

A number of the students could be seen making side notes in their course binders.

Mark proceeded by restating the question that had been asked last week. He wrote a summary of the solution on the board, and listed the points that needed to be addressed to implement it. Seeing that the students all seemed to understand the steps, he further clarified it by showing how to use the software tools on the computer to come up with a complete solution.

All of the students were nodding their heads by this time.

"OK, class. Now let's start to review the material that you will need to know for the exam. Who can tell me what a data warehouse is?"

"It's a warehouse with data in it."

"It's a building with information in it."

"It's a building with computers in it."

Mark sighed and held up his hand. "You cannot just use the question as the answer or change the words in the question," he said.

"A data warehouse is actually a specialized database of pre-calculated totals that is used by management to quickly get reports that show patterns in their business's activities."

"I knew that," Marcia said. Mark could barely restrain himself from rolling his eyes.

"On the exam, you will have to demonstrate that you know what the required concepts are and also how to apply them. You will see some definition questions like I just asked you. You will also be expected to know the differences between concepts, the methods that can be used to implement them, and how to apply those methods in business problems that will be given to you."

"That sounds like a lot."

"These are all of the basic skills that businesses will expect you to know when they hire you.

"I would also like to suggest that you determine the maximum amount of time that you can spend on each question in the exam. For instance, if a question is only worth 10 % of the total exam marks then don't spend any more than 10 % of the total exam time working on it. Otherwise, you will run out of time on the exam and you will rush through questions that are worth more points.

"Let's try another question. What is the difference between RAD development and SDLC development?"

"One is a newer method and the other is an older method," said Tim.

"That is correct but it does not prove that you understand what they are. That is like saying that an airplane is newer than a car. You need to tell me how each of them work, or what their purpose is.

"Your answers need to be detailed enough so that they can clearly demonstrate your knowledge of the material in the current course.

"You must carefully read each question in the test, in order to put down the appropriate material that will answer it. You must also come up with precise answers, and not several contradictory answers."

Mark then tried a few other basic questions. The students were starting to get the idea.

"Now that you understand the details that will be required on the exam, I will list out the questions that were sent to me and then go over the material that is relevant to them. I will also add in other topics that you will have to know for the exam." As Mark listed the topics on the board he could see that all of the students were paying attention now.

"Does anyone else have any other review topics that they would like to see listed on the board?"

"I would like to know more about the techniques that we can use for managing supply chains. I plan to work in that area, and it was covered briefly at the beginning of this course."

"OK. That is a good idea. It could be used to solve one of the business problems in the exam, instead of some of the other techniques that I will be discussing."

"Why don't you just tell us what the questions are in the exam, and then we'll know exactly what to study for?" one of the students suggested.

"Ha! Nice try. What I can do is tell you what is not going to be on the exam. The other topics in the course, including what I have listed on the board, may or may not be on the exam. This will allow you to focus on the important concepts during your studying."

Cheering erupted in the class.

Mark referred to the course textbook, and to his notes, and spent the next few minutes listing out all of the topics that could not be tested in the exam due to its time constraints. When he was done he made sure to point out to his students, "You may still have to know this material at some of the businesses where you will eventually work. It is still useful to review it."

"Your list is not long enough. Keep writing."

"If I make it any longer then all of you will be out of the exam in half the time."

"We don't mind. Every little bit helps."

Mark decided that he could add a few more topics to his list on the board. There were still enough topics left for him to review, so that the exam could comprehensively test his students on the fundamental methods that were covered in the course. The students would need to know these at every business where they might work.

He proceeded to go through each of the required topics on the board. He started by summarizing the notes that he had previously covered for each of them, and then he showed some solutions on how to apply the material.

Finally, he gave a problem for each of the topics and asked the students to suggest solutions for the problems. He told them to consider the business processes for financial systems, for payment systems, and for the various marketing approaches. He also told them to consider technological processes such as electronic commerce systems, networks, security systems, database structures, various application software and the various types of computer systems.

By the time that the class was done, all of the students were smiling and in a good mood. He felt confident that all of them would do well on the exam next week.

"So, how is everyone feeling? Are you more comfortable with the course material now?"

"That was great! I wish that more instructors conducted their classes the way that you do."

Mark didn't know what to say. He was just applying his work experience to what he had learned, so that he could share relevant methods with the students. He thought that everyone did that at some point.

As the class wrapped up and the students headed off to their next classes, he started thinking about what the students had said, and about how well the class had gone that day.

That evening, he began writing his ideas down on what worked and what didn't work in the classrooms. He had seen many administrative and governmental changes over the last few years that were affecting the quality of education. He had also seen many different instructor styles, as well as changes in student attitudes towards education.

He organized his ideas into administrative issues, classroom issues, and course preparation requirements. He also added in his suggestions for conducting efficient courses in such a way that they would be beneficial for the students later on in their careers.

Over the next few weeks, those ideas were expanded into the details for the first book that he published. It presented his observations on changes that he had seen over the years that had affected the quality of education, along with his recommendations for changes that were needed to protect the future and value of education.

He wanted to ensure that all students could obtain as much practical knowledge and skills as possible during their time in university, so that they would be fully prepared for their chosen careers.

Later that year he went on a cruise where he started thinking about more topics that he could share with others. When he came back from that cruise, he started to organize the notes from his graduate and doctoral courses, from the notes that he had developed for the courses that he taught, and from his work experiences on applying what he had learned over the years. Those evolved over the next year into another series of books to show business people, as well as technical people, how to exploit relevant concepts in their operations.

Mark discovered that fateful day that the students had changed his life and the way that he thought about education, just as he was having an impact on their lives.

As he began thinking about the best way to test their knowledge of all of the topics, he vowed that he would also try to encourage positive changes in the education system from his writings, and from the example that he set in his own classrooms.

That evening, he also reflected back on his own studies and on the way that he had been taught.

Chapter 6: Past Challenges

Wisdom begins in wonder. (Socrates)

When Mark had attended courses at his undergraduate university, he did not question the difficulty of those courses. He thought that all university courses were like that. Each of his courses was conducted by a professor who presented a ton of notes each class on the board, handed out lots of reading to do, and then handed out several long complex assignments to do.

The tests from the professors were also quite detailed, and it took a long time to complete them. On top of that, the marking of the tests and assignments was very strict, as the professors expected the students to live up to very high standards.

Upon graduation, Mark found that several companies were eager to hire him and his fellow graduates, in order to take advantage of their current knowledge of technological and business processes.

He used to hate all of his professors but he found out that everything that he was asked to do in various businesses was easy, compared to the intensity and complexity of the assignments that he had completed in university.

He was even able to pass several industry certifications with relative ease, due to the intense training in the courses that he had taken.

He often heard the phrase, *you can pay me now or you can pay me later.*

There were no evaluations of professors when he had attended university, and so they were under no obligations to make their courses easy, in order to get excellent evaluation grades. They also did not feel that they had to pass the students.

Mark had sweated through every one of his courses, wondering if he would get good grades in them. He could not argue with his professors or the university, at that time, in order to try to increase his grades on the tests and assignments.

He was sure that he would have given every one of his professors a low evaluation due to the tests being too hard, the assignments being too hard, the marking being too strict, too much reading being assigned, or too many notes being given. At least, that was what he thought.

Looking back, he realized that his time in the university had prepared him quite well for his working life. For sure, there was still a lot of material that was taught that he could not use.

However, he felt that he would have struggled later on when he had tried to find a company to hire him, and then struggled again to do the jobs that they required him to do, if there were evaluations at that time, and if his professors had been replaced by those who were easier on the students.

His master's studies actually turned out to be more manageable, which was good for him since he was working during the day, attending his classes in the evening, and then doing his assignments on the weekend. There were still no evaluations of professors at that time, at least for the university that he had attended, but at least the professors gave you a special course manual with all of the notes in it. All of the assignments and tests were based on applying the material to actual business situations, which was exactly what Mark was doing during the day at his consulting job.

Many universities were moving to case studies for masters programs, since the professors found that it was a better way for the students to appreciate the advanced topics and how they could be used.

Mark often wondered at that time, '*Why don't the universities take that approach with undergraduate studies?*'

He made a note to teach that way, with lots of industry examples, if he ever got the chance to teach classes. That opportunity was actually presented to him a few months after he finally graduated with his master's degree.

He left his consulting job when he was offered a full-time job with one of the local universities. It would mean that he could now work regular hours, he could have his evenings and weekends available for himself, and he wouldn't have to fly all over the country to consult with multiple clients. Of course, he didn't count on all of the time that he would have to spend learning new business processes and computer technologies for his courses each term, as he was to discover later.

Mark was very popular the first week that he began teaching classes at a university. He did not have any teaching experience, and so he conducted his classes as if his students were consultants. He would come to class as if he was attending a meeting of the executives for a business. His dressing was very formal.

He would usually show up in three piece suits, but on occasion he would dress down a little bit and wear a two piece suit. His ties always had a clasp on them. His crisp white shirts had cufflinks on them. The breast pocket of his jacket had a folded handkerchief in it. The lapel of his jacket had a pin on it from one of his numerous certifications.

He tried to show his students how to apply the course material to solve different business situations. He had a wealth of material to draw on from his working experience, and from his frequent travels to other countries.

Most of the other instructors were teaching the material *as is* from the textbooks, but Mark spent time finding actual business examples that could help to illustrate the concepts in his courses. His students could then easily grasp the material as it was presented.

Mark still had to present everything in the textbooks for the official course outlines, but he was able to make the material more relevant to his students. His assignments were then based on solving problems that he had seen while consulting with businesses.

One of the first courses that he was asked to teach was a database class. He assumed that the university had a separate computer system for all of their courses, and so he gave every one of his students an administrator account. He then encouraged them to experiment with the course material to understand it better.

He received a frantic call later that week from the administrators at the university.

"What have your students done?" someone shouted at him through the phone.

The entire campus had to be shutdown. Its computer systems had suddenly stopped. It took some time to figure out what the problem was, but it was determined that it was Mark's students that had done it. Mark had to restrict their privileges by locking them into a single database.

He learned a valuable lesson that week. Do not make assumptions! When the next term started, he noticed that the university had now given all students their own computer systems.

Another course that he was asked to teach in his first term was so popular that the university had to schedule him to teach three sessions of it, back to back. The classrooms could only hold so many students, and so three classrooms were needed to accommodate all of the students who wanted to take the course.

Each class was two hours long for that course. The university scheduled him to teach the class at 8 AM, at 10 AM, and at 1 PM. He seriously considered that he should have just video recorded his lecture at 8 AM, and then simply played it back for his other two classes.

However, all classes are slightly different, and so he personally conducted the lectures for each of the classes. He ended up adjusting the material that he taught, based on the backgrounds of his students, and on the questions that they asked.

In the middle of his first term, he received a call from the dean of his department.

"Hi Mark. One of our instructors has to leave for a week to attend to a family emergency. Would you be able to cover his classes next week?"

"Did he leave any notes that I can refer to?"

"He is just using the slides from the publisher of the book that we use for that course."

Mark readily agreed to cover the classes, but he did not want to just present slides. A trained monkey could simply present slides. Mark was not a fan of just reading the material on slides, and then expecting the students to magically absorb the material that they had seen on the slides.

He had seen slides used effectively in businesses to summarize activities, but not in classrooms where the students were expected to grasp the details of a course, in order to use those details in their jobs later on. When only slides were used in a classroom, then the students would just attempt to read them on their own, and then the students would not even bother coming to the classes.

Mark felt that the students needed to be told what the important points were, among all of the material that was presented. They needed to understand the importance of specific concepts, and how it could be used to solve business problems. They deserved to take courses that got them involved in their studies so that they could more clearly understand the required material.

Mark spent the upcoming weekend reviewing the course textbook and what the students were supposed to be learning in the course that he was to cover. It dealt with topics on using a computer operating system that was popular among scientists. More and more businesses had also started using it in recent years. It had a more robust security system, and lower operating costs, but its commands were much more complex than those used by most business operating systems.

The book for the course mentioned the benefits of the system and listed the commands that it used. It did not cover any details on how to use the commands or on how to setup the system to make it work properly.

Mark remedied this by making up notes on configuration files, command options, security setups, network access methods, file editing options, and backup scheduling. He also made up examples for the materials, along with some exercises that he could give to the students that would help to clarify their application of the materials.

When he went into the classroom for this course on Monday afternoon, he noticed that half of the students were missing for the course, according to the class registration list that he had been given.

"Good afternoon. I am Professor Mark Klepin. I just joined the university and I am currently teaching their courses on databases and system design. I spent several years before this consulting with various businesses around the world. I have designed and built a variety of systems, and I hope that I can share some of that knowledge with you this week."

He apologized for the absence of their regular instructor. He mentioned that he would not be using the slides from the book's publisher because they did not provide enough detail to be useful. He then proceeded with listing a summary of the topics that he would be discussing that week.

As the lecture proceeded, he got the students to use their computers to try out the commands that he was showing them on the board. He wandered among them to help them out, in order to be sure that everyone understood the material.

The next day, he was pleasantly surprised to see that every single student on the registration list had shown up for his lecture. Word had apparently gotten around concerning the details of the material that he was covering in his lectures.

At the end of the week, a student approached him and said, "Professor Klepin, I feel that I've learned more from you in one week than I've learned from reading the entire course textbook."

Mark replied, "That is why learning is such a dynamic environment. It is why the universities prefer to use classrooms, instead of just asking the students to read a book to figure it out on their own. Students deserve to be taught."

Evaluations were being introduced in the first term that he taught, and he was surprised when he got high evaluations. There was still a lot of reading and work to do in all of his courses. His fellow instructors were not so lucky, and several got replaced by those who were even easier on the students in the courses.

Between his first two terms, he was also sent over to the offices of a large security organization. They had arranged for the university to send someone over for a week. They wanted to know how to use computer software to look for patterns in the data in their databases. They said that this would allow them to do their jobs more effectively. Mark got picked to go over to them due to his extensive consulting background from before he had joined the university.

He spent a day reviewing various software tools, and then he designed a week long mini-course for teaching data analysis concepts. He focused on research methods, database query commands, statistical analysis techniques, and graphical presentation styles. He also made up some relevant situations that he could use to illustrate concepts, along with instructions for using the software tools.

When he arrived at the security organization, he was escorted to a large room that they used for strategic meetings. There was a row of computer terminals along the back wall, and a terminal and projector at the front for a speaker. Several tables and chairs were arranged facing the front of the room. The chairs were already filled with security officials. Every one of them was wearing a sidearm.

'I guess that I'd better do a good job of teaching them,' Mark thought nervously.

In the first day that he taught them, he was shocked when several individuals in full combat gear entered the room, in order to use the terminals along the back wall. He was told that he would probably see some others over the next few days, since he was teaching in a shared strategy room. This unnerved him a little, especially when the combat professionals hung around to listen to his lectures. But the course went well, and the university administrators sent him over there a few more times between the terms that he taught in later years.

In his second term of teaching at the university, he had a student register in his database course that was shown on his class lists as an auditor. He placed a call to the administration office to inquire on this. They called him back to tell him that the student had just arrived in the country, and that she had told them that she was thinking about attending their university.

"What does auditing my course mean? I am not familiar with that term, except when it is used in the business world to verify financial amounts."

"It means that she's allowed to attend the course unofficially. We are hoping that she'll like our campus environment. If she likes you and your course then she'll be enrolling full-time with us in the next term."

After the term was over, this lady approached Mark and asked him if she could *audit* him. Her name was Natalia and she became his second wife. She ended up helping out her sister to start a successful business, and she never did attend further university courses due to her focus on growing that business.

Natalia was a wonderful lady and she had a great influence on his life over the next few years.

Mark actually credited his pursuit of doctoral studies to her. She said to him one day, "You teach in a university now. You should study more and get a PhD."

This was a completely opposite opinion than that given to him by his first wife, who had told him to just stop studying and to only work.

"I could do that but I'm worried about all of the time that it would take away from us."

"Don't worry. I'll help you out in every way that I can. Just get it done. It's better to endure some pain for two or three years rather than dragging it out for several years. My parents, and yours, will be so proud of you when you get it."

He reluctantly agreed. He thought that he had done enough studying in his life already. He was not sure what the benefits were since he was already accepted by the university as one of their instructors.

First he approached the university administrators to see if they were still willing to pay for his doctoral studies. They told him that they were but that they could only give him a few thousand dollars each year towards it. However, as long as he continued teaching for the university after getting his PhD, then they would continue paying him this amount every year until his doctoral studies were fully paid for.

This sounded fair to Mark.

Next he had to find universities that would accept an MBA degree for credit towards a PhD degree. Most of the universities considered an MBA as a terminal, or final, degree. A few universities had created DBA programs for a Doctor of Business Administration, but a PhD was the coveted degree among all of the universities, and so Mark was determined to get it.

He also wanted to find a university that would allow him to combine business topics with technology topics. Most of the universities specialized in one type of degree or the other.

He ended up finding three universities that fit his criteria. They offered PhD's in Business and Technology. Two of the universities were public institutions run by the governments but one was a private university. He checked further and found out that the private university was accredited by a well-respected governing body, and so its degrees would be recognized by other universities.

Mark asked his wife for advice, "What do you think Natalia?"

She replied, "The private one is only half the cost of the public ones. Even though your university is paying for the cost, you would be able to leave them sooner if you got a better opportunity somewhere else." She was already thinking about the future and was making plans for him.

"My feelings are that the public ones have a better image than the private one but I can see your point."

Based on her feelings, he enrolled in the private university and he started his doctoral studies later that year. The university had already agreed to let him do his research at the university where he was teaching, with periodic visits to them to track his research, and to plan out the courses that he would need each term.

Due to his acceptance into doctoral studies, his own university offered him a faculty chair position while he was working on it. He would be assisting the dean in scheduling other faculty and in designing new courses. It was a great opportunity! It also meant that he could cut back on the number of courses that he was teaching himself so that he could focus on his new studies.

While he had the faculty chair position, he developed a system to identify the main teaching resource for each course, plus two backup resources. When possible, he tried to identify quality instructors that had a variety of skills who could cover many types of courses. He only used the backup resources if his main teaching resources could not cover a course.

In this manner, Mark built up expertise for all of the courses that he scheduled. He was able to consolidate several positions into new full time positions, minimize the use of part time instructors, and to lower the payroll costs for the university. He ended up with a department that was easier to manage, the instructors working for him were now more loyal, and the instructors were constantly kept busy with courses.

His first term with the private university was overloaded with advanced courses in business and technology, plus a research course that taught him sophisticated techniques on how to find the related research that others were doing, and on how to analyze and present results. It was almost too much for him, given all of the preparation that he also had to do for the courses that he was currently teaching.

"Natalia, after this term, I think that I'd like to withdraw from the PhD program. It is too much. I'd rather spend all of my time with you. I feel like I am back in my undergraduate times again. I think that I just want to teach my own courses now, and not have to study even more courses."

"Don't you dare do that! I support you. I know that you can do it. It'll only be for a couple of years if you focus carefully on your studies and on your assignments."

Mark hung in and managed to finish his first term with excellent grades. His only shock came when the private university gave him and the other students a letter that their fees would be jumping 20 % in their next term. They said that it was because they had now become accredited by an international business association, and so there was more administration involved. They noted that their degrees would also be more prestigious now.

This fee increase infuriated Mark. He turned to his wife and said, "Look what they have done! I think that I should withdraw. This is ridiculous!"

She thought about it for a moment, and then replied, "It's definitely a rather large increase, but their costs are still lower than the public universities that you had told me about. I suggest that you just bear with it and then continue with your studies."

The following day that he was teaching, he was so distracted by the fee increase for his own studies that he pulled out the wrong set of notes for one of his classes. The notes were for his class later that day, but he managed to lecture for a full 30 minutes before one of his students put up his hand. "Excuse me sir, what does this material have to do with the topics in this course?"

Mark realized that most of the students in his class looked confused. A few of them just had blank looks on their faces. He could not believe that he had been so distracted that he had taught them from the wrong notes. He also couldn't believe that it took 30 minutes before the students realized that the topic was unrelated to their studies.

'Maybe they assumed that there was a connection in the material somewhere to what they were studying?' he thought.

'Probably they were just waking up this early in the morning,' he finally assumed.

"I was just kidding with you. Now that I know that you are paying attention, let's continue with the correct materials this time," he said. Mark made a note to himself to be more careful in the future.

"Very funny, sir," another one of his students added as a final remark.

Over the next year Mark continued with his studies. He had to submit several major papers during that time as part of his doctoral degree. The first one was a concept paper that outlined the research that he would like to do, why his research was significant, and some of the related research that others were doing.

He wanted to develop a new method that could compare the complexity of different computer technologies, and that could reveal the innate reasons for those complexities.

He also had to choose whether he would be doing quantitative or qualitative research. Quantitative research focused on analyzing results with statistics while qualitative research focused on finding patterns in research data. Mark was feeling brave and he wanted to try both.

His concept paper was accepted with great enthusiasm by the university, and then a committee was formed to guide the rest of his research. The committee was guided by a chair person, who was a professor that was knowledgeable in the type of research that he would be doing. The committee also consisted of two other professors that would monitor his research to ensure that it was conducted in the proper manner.

Mark received a shock when the committee chair person rejected the concept paper that the university itself had just accepted. Apparently, the chair person had his own way of doing things, and he therefore wanted all of Mark's research ideas from the last several months redone.

Mark pounded the table at his home in frustration when he opened the letter from his committee. Natalia came over to console him. "What is it now, Mark?"

"Now they want me to redo all of the work that I've done. But the university has already accepted the ideas in my concept paper."

"Calm down. Just call the university tomorrow and contact the dean of the department. He controls the professors and he can remind them about the university's regulations. The committee cannot deny your research topic when the university has already approved it."

Natalia's mother had been a teacher, and later an administrator back in her country. Natalia knew a few things about how education systems worked, or were supposed to work.

Mark nervously placed a call the next day. He had a long chat first with the dean of the department, who then got Mark's committee involved. They all finally agreed that Mark could continue his research for the topic that he had identified, and in the ways that he wanted.

The next paper that he produced was the prospectus that identified who he would be conducting his research on, how he would be collecting his research data, and some annotated references from at least 100 other researchers who were conducting similar research. He identified that he would be doing his research on students at the university where he taught, as previously approved by the private university when he had enrolled with them.

His committee rejected his prospectus! They wanted him to expand his research to include all students at all universities in the country. This was overwhelming, expensive, and would take him years to conduct. Normally, only a national study that was funded by a federal research council would be this comprehensive.

His wife rushed over when she saw him starting to bang his head on the table.

"Talk to me Mark. What's happened?"

"Look at this. How can I do this? This goes way beyond what doctoral students are supposed to do. It sounds like they want me to do their own research for them."

"You have to fight this. This is wrong."

Mark spent that night composing his thoughts and arguments.

The next day, he started with his student academic advisor, and then moved on to the dean of the department at the private university, then to the president, and finally he managed to reach the provost of the university (who is the Chief Academic Officer for a university).

The provost intervened on his behalf and agreed that his committee had overstepped their bounds. It was agreed by everyone that he could just add the students from one more university to his research, in order to minimize any bias in his results.

Approval was also needed at this time from an ethics committee at the university. They wanted to make sure that he was not torturing students, or putting them in stressful situations.

Most researchers collected research data by doing experiments in labs, by doing surveys, or by conducting observations of activities. Mark was just asking some students to develop computer software, and some others to then evaluate that software. The committee approved his research, which was of an immense relief to him.

He spent the next two months writing up a proposal paper. This represented about half of what would be in a doctoral dissertation paper. It presented the problem that he was investigating, the ways that others had approached the problem (called a literary review), and extensive quotes from their research. It also included the methodology that he was using, that explained where he would collect his research data from, and how he would conduct his research.

Thankfully, his committee accepted it and the dean of the department also accepted it. The university then issued him a letter that he was now officially a doctoral candidate. He could now proceed with collecting and analyzing his research data, write it all up in a dissertation paper, and go on to defend his research before another committee.

He was overjoyed! He spent the weekend celebrating with his wife, and was definitely not prepared for the news that he then received the following week from the private university.

They issued a letter to all students that they were raising their rates another 50 %! They said that they had underestimated all of their costs due to all of the accreditations that they had obtained, in order to improve their reputation even further.

Now Mark was beyond furious! He wondered how this could even be legal. He still had at least two more terms to complete with the university.

He thought, '*I should've just chosen one of the public universities to study my PhD with, and taken advantage of their already established reputation.*'

He was ready to just give up. He started thinking that maybe their rates would jump again in the next term. He still had to collect and analyze his research data, and then to defend it. Other doctoral students had told him that a university could drag this out for several terms.

"Natalia, I think that I need to rethink the value of a PhD. It could cost me a small fortune to finish it."

"What do you mean? I thought that you were doing well and that you're almost finished it."

"The university just raised its rates by 50 %. I should be finished within two more terms, but my committee could easily cause me to spend several more terms completing my dissertation. I'm worried that the university will have another huge rate increase, or several, before I'm done."

"Mark, they have you now and they know it. Doctoral dissertations can't be transferred to other universities. I suggest that you just do the best that you can over the next few months and then get your PhD finished. I'm confident in your abilities."

It took Mark a few months to finally collect all of his research data from the students at two universities. He found it difficult to obtain students who were willing to participate, as well as to coordinate the many meetings that were required with them.

He started by posting advertisements on the bulletin boards at the university where he worked, and on those at the other university that he had been asked to include in his research as well. His own students were eager to participate but those at the other university did not know him. They were wary of participating in any research study.

Maybe the students thought that Mark was going to torture them?

There was a notification of informed consent form that all participants in research studies had to sign. It outlined their responsibilities and the purpose of the research. Mark lost a few students when they realized that they would have to sign a form, and then actually do something.

Whenever several students contacted him in the same week, he would book rooms at the university to put them into, in order to make his research seem more official. It took a while but Mark finally obtained all of the research data that he needed.

Once he started analyzing all of the data that he had collected, he realized that he had become very good at statistics. He had hated it in his undergraduate studies, hated it even more in his master's studies, but now he was using it extensively in his doctoral studies, even though he still hated it.

He managed to get through the statistical analysis of his data and was able to make some decent conclusions from it. He wrote it all up, added it to his proposal paper, and created a dissertation paper for his committee. He was so proud of his dissertation paper.

It was rejected! It turned out that dissertation papers don't get a grade like regular assignments. They have to be perfect! So committees will keep rejecting them until they feel that they are perfect. Mark learned later that some of the other doctoral students had submitted papers a dozen times before their committees had finally accepted their dissertation papers.

Mark's paper was full of comments on almost every page. He wondered, *'Why didn't they just tell me what they wanted before I submitted it?'*

He spent the next week adding in all of the corrections that the committee wanted, and it was rejected again. The paper was full of more comments. *'Here we go again,'* he thought.

By the fifth time that this happened, he blew up. He asked the committee to just tell him up front the full details of everything that they wanted so that he could complete it. He was quite annoyed with them, and his language was very harsh.

He ended up with a committee that would not talk to him for two months. They wanted to withdraw from supporting him. He did not think that they were doing a very good of supporting him so far anyway.

He asked his fellow doctoral students what to do. They said that if a committee withdraws then he would have to start his entire PhD all over again. No committee would jump in to help a student to complete a dissertation when it was almost done.

Mark felt that he had reached the end of his rope. He didn't know how many more times he would have to perfect his dissertation paper.

Once again, he commiserated with his wife, "Natalia, I've been spending every night and every weekend for the last two years working on this PhD. It's hard on you and it's wiping me out. I can't see any more when it's going to end."

"You need to have personal conversations with all of your committee members and sort this out. You are so close. Please don't give up. You know that I'll always stand behind you to encourage you onwards."

As it turned out, it also took conversations with the president of the private university again, as well as its provost, but he finally got back on track with his dissertation. Within another couple of tries, his dissertation was accepted. He was now ready to move on to defend the research in it and the conclusions that he had made in it.

The defense of a dissertation is performed in a room before a special committee that is made up of the original committee, the dean of the department, and a professor from another university. It can go on for hours as they ask candidates to justify the various parts of their dissertation.

A single dissatisfied committee member can stop a PhD process cold, and force the candidate to redo all of the research. This normally only happens if some underlying research has been discredited since it was originally published. Usually, dissertations are accepted *as is* or with some minor corrections, such as more statistical analysis.

On the day of his dissertation defense, Mark was fidgeting and sweating profusely.

"So tell us Mark, in one sentence, what was the significance of your research?"

Mark proceeded to ramble on for over two minutes until he was out of breath.

"Wow! That was the longest sentence that I have ever heard in my life but it is acceptable. Now please explain the conclusions that you have made from your statistical analysis."

That took considerably longer. The committee members were all nodding their heads so Mark assumed that he was off to a good start.

"Now tell us why the sample size for your research is so small. We were expecting several hundred participants."

This required that he carefully explain about alpha levels, power levels, effect sizes, correlations, and within-subject studies. He was sure that he would pass out from all of the water that was leaving his body from sweating.

Over the next hour, there were also questions about the related research that others had done, the methods that he had chosen to do his analysis, and on how his research could be expanded on by others.

Finally they told him, "Mark, we all agree that we will accept your research *as is*, or perhaps we should now say Doctor Mark Klepin."

It took him a moment to realize that they had called him Doctor! He staggered over to a nearby chair and collapsed into it. He had his PhD!

After vigorously shaking everyone's hands, he rushed home. His wife had already heard the great news and had managed to organize a big party for him with a few friends, in order to greet him when he arrived home.

Even at the university the next day where he was teaching, the students had heard the news and they had organized a big party for him as well. They spent the day going around calling him *Doctor* whenever they met him in the hallways. Some of them were even saluting him.

Later that week, he reflected on the last two years from his doctoral studies, on his master's studies, and on his undergraduate studies. He did not ever want students to go through what he had.

He would be careful in the future to organize all of his materials and he would tell students exactly what was expected of them. He would continue giving them examples that would enhance their learning, so that they could easily handle complex assignments or complex tests. He wanted his students to be fully prepared for whatever their working lives threw at them.

A few months after he obtained his PhD, he attended the formal graduation ceremonies for it. The ceremonies were held in a historic stone building that was reminiscent of a palace. Rich tapestries adorned its central hall.

All of the doctoral graduates were given elegant gowns to wear. The gowns were of a rich dark green color that was made of soft cashmere wool. They had bright gold stripes along the front with billowing sleeves. At the back was a royal blue cape of thick wool. Mark felt that all he needed to complete his ensemble was a colonial wig and a gold medallion around his neck. He felt like a king!

His parents and his wife's parents were present for his graduation. His father commented to him that he was immensely proud of everything that Mark had accomplished in his work and in his studies. He expressed his misgivings that he had not given him more support in his early years. He promised to help him out now in any way that he could.

Mark was further honored by being chosen to give the convocation address for his fellow graduates. He compared the doctoral process to training for Olympic quality fencing. There were many trials and tribulations along the way while proper techniques were learned and enforced. Mental and emotional bruises were often left, just like the physical bruises from fencing. But the intense training prepared oneself for any future situations that one might encounter. The training also instilled in oneself the desire to continually strive for higher excellence in all that one did in life.

Mark thought that his hard times were all behind him now, and that his teaching could proceed more smoothly from this point on. He looked forward to helping students obtain their dreams and he did not anticipate any more difficulties, or so he hoped.

Chapter 7: The Reflection

Easy to learn, hard to master. (Lao Tzu)

Mark's review of the course material with his students earlier in the week had seemed to go better than he had expected. The students were struggling earlier in the term with the course, but now everyone appeared to be grasping the material.

Over the weekend, Mark would try to think about the best way to verify that his students understood the material in his current course. He wanted to create a test that could stand up to public scrutiny.

His goal was to create a test that could potentially be posted in a national newspaper. This could be used to show the public the high quality of standards that were being upheld in a properly designed course. It would prove that the students' knowledge of material was being properly verified. It would also make business people aware of all of the material that students were being taught to master. This would create a higher demand for students when they graduated. Businesses would be more eager to utilize the students' advanced skill sets.

First Mark decided to set down some basic rules for the test. *'I want the students to have a clear idea of how the midterm exam will be graded,'* he reflected.

He decided that he would start off by stating that the students could not just use the questions as the answers, as he had pointed out to them during his review. He expanded on this by stating that his questions could not be used as the answers to the other questions later on.

He had seen cases in previous terms where the students simply took all of his definition questions, and then put them in later as the solution to some business problem. There was a lot of other material in his courses that they could utilize.

He liked to encourage students to *think outside the box*, and then to use any of the course material to solve the problems that were given to them.

He also decided that he didn't want to see students putting down the same answer multiple times in the test. This only proved that they knew the one concept when they kept repeating it. He could only give credit for an answer once. He needed to verify that the students also knew of the other concepts that were taught in the course.

For that matter, he did not want them putting down more answers than the questions required. This would mean that they were just guessing, and that they were putting down as much material from the course as they could, in the hope that some of it was correct. In those cases, he could not give them credit when many contradictory answers were given.

Finally, he would recommend on the exam paper that all of their calculation steps should be shown. In that way, he could still award part marks if most of the work was correct, but the student had simply miscalculated a step. Otherwise, if he only had a final answer, then he could only give full marks for a correct answer or a zero for an incorrect answer. This was one of the reasons that he never did multiple choice tests.

He wanted to give the students every opportunity to earn marks. He did not want them simply guessing at the answers.

Once he had determined the basic rules for his test, he considered the types of questions that he would need to ask the students. He didn't want to have just one type of question, such as only definitions. He needed to be sure that the students understood the concepts in the course and that they could apply them.

This reminded him. He needed to check up on the students in his online course. He usually supervised one or two of these online courses every term. Besides the chat rooms and emails, he had set up a virtual office hour each week when the students could have a live talk with him.

He put on his headset, activated his web camera, and connected to his online course. There were already several students waiting for him. Most students came from the surrounding areas but there were always a few students from other countries that were enrolled in the online courses.

"There you are. We were just chatting amongst ourselves and wondering where you were," one of the students said.

"Sorry. I was busy designing some test rules for my campus course."

"Do our tests have any rules that we should know about?"

Mark proceeded to explain the rules to them.

"Your tests can be taken at any time in the week that they are scheduled for. Once the week is over then you cannot take the test. They have a time limit once you start them, the same as my campus courses. However, everyone gets different questions when they take them. The computer will randomly pull out questions from the textbook so that you can't share questions and answers with each other. This is because you are allowed to write the tests at any time of the week."

"Did you make up those questions, Professor?" another student asked.

"All of the questions come from the publisher of the textbook and they are marked by the computer and not by me. All of the reading assignments come from the textbook. Any slides or videos that you have seen have come from the publisher of the textbook. For that matter, all of the examples also come from the textbook and all of your assignments come from the textbook."

"Why don't you make up a video for us or give us some stories from your consulting career?" the same student suggested to him.

Mark had to be careful about how he replied. He knew that all of the video conversations, chat conversations, and email conversations within online courses were closely monitored by the administrators at a university.

"That is because the university wants all of their online courses to be consistent, regardless of who is teaching it. I have a lot more flexibility in my campus courses. I often make up notes from projects that I have worked on. I can also make up assignments that are based on them, and I can construct tests that focus only on those concepts that businesses require students to know. Another nice point of campus courses is that I am able to respond immediately to questions as the material is being taught."

"I have a question. Can you explain the material in Chapter 8 to us?"

"It would take me more than one hour to do that. Live lectures are not part of online classes. Students are expected to learn the material on their own from the assigned readings and from any notes or slides that are posted. However, if you have a specific question then I can address it during this office hour or in the chat rooms."

"I was hoping that I wouldn't have to read the material by myself. I guess that I'm more used to taking courses at a campus than taking courses online," the student commented to him.

"You are not alone in your thoughts. Many students find that online courses are harder and more time consuming than campus courses. The online courses require a lot more self-discipline to complete successfully. Plus you have mandatory discussions that you must do. You cannot just remain silent like you can do in a campus course.

"On top of this, you must usually pass each section of an online course. You must pass the discussion sections, the testing sections, the assignment sections, and the final exam section. Most universities do not simply take an average of all of the sections. You have to prove to the university from your actions that it is you taking the course and not your friends taking it for you."

"I am taking the course myself, Professor. Honest. Trust me. While we have you, can you check out the settings on my computer? I'm having a lot of trouble getting the software to do what the book wants me to do."

Mark found that one of the cool features of online courses was his ability to remotely take control of any of his students' computers to check their settings or to guide them through a specific problem that they were having. He was able to see this student's problem as soon as he checked up on it.

"Your problem is all fixed now. It was due to a setting that you had saved in your last assignment. The book did mention that that setting had to be reset before starting the next assignment."

"Thanks, Professor."

"You're welcome. But this is why I like to teach students in the classroom or in the labs. It allows me to save students countless hours of study time. But I realize that some of you are working. Online courses give you considerable flexibility for course times. You can still get exposed to new subject areas by taking online courses."

Mark knew that many universities required that students accept a memorandum of understanding for online courses before they were even allowed access to them. The deadlines for tests and assignments had firm cut off dates. The students had an entire week to hand them in before this. Assignments could be handed in even earlier and some students did them all in the first month of a course. However, once a deadline was reached then the students were expected to understand that they could not give excuses to try to hand in assignments even later, or to retake tests that they had missed.

The final exam for online courses was often proctored (supervised) at a fixed time at any nearby college or university.

Some online courses had a fixed time when students could access the course to do a final exam on the university's computer before a cut off time was reached.

The rest of Mark's virtual office hour went smoothly. He found that most students in online courses preferred to just use the public chat rooms to ask questions or to email him privately with their questions.

After an hour, he was ready to get back to designing his own exam for his campus students.

'I guess that I'll start out with some definitions to get them thinking about the material,' he thought.

'Next I can ask them to explain the differences between related concepts so that they need to think about the advantages and disadvantages of each of them when they're using them to solve problems.'

He realized that some of the topics in the course had multiple methods that he had been taught for them. For those, he would just ask the students to identify any three methods within them that could be used to construct solutions for businesses.

He also needed to test the students on the details of at least a couple of the methods that he had covered extensively in the course. He would then need to think up some problems that they could do some calculations on.

He concluded that he could also ask his class to draw a diagram that described a business situation that he would give to them. He had covered many diagrams in this term already.

Finally, he would need a wrap up question that would allow the students to use several parts of the course to solve a business problem. This would give them the opportunity to use any topic that they were most comfortable with.

Mark decided that he needed a break at this point.

There was a computer show downtown that had just started this weekend. So he hopped in his car and headed down there to check it out. One of his students was already there and spotted him when he got there. The student came over to chat with him.

"Hey, Professor Klepin! Isn't this cool? Can you show us in class how to use some of this technology?"

"That is one of the reasons why I came down here Edward. I want to get some ideas for doing just that. Let's walk around and look at some of the exhibits."

There were so many exhibits that it was overwhelming. Mark headed up to the second floor to get to a balcony that overlooked the exhibit area. From there, he was able to see how the different technology areas were arranged, in order to plan out a route to visit the more interesting ones.

As he explored the various exhibits, some of the vendors started giving him samples of their products as gifts. Many of them also gave him their business cards, especially when Edward told them that he taught technology subjects at the university. The vendors were hoping that he would pick up their technology, and then show it to his students. Edward took advantage of these meetings to also pass along his resume to the vendors in the hope that he could get some part-time or full-time work out of it.

After an hour, Mark asked Edward if he would mind carrying all of the gifts that he had received. "You will owe me a favor," said Edward, but he willingly helped to carry everything.

Mark found that the time that he had spent so far at the computer show was very rewarding. However, after another hour he collected his gifts from Edward and thanked him. He decided that he would have to come back next week to talk to some of the vendors in more detail.

A short drive later, he finally got back to his home.

"Time to go through the course notes to make up the test questions," he said to himself.

He did not like to make up questions that were based on the textbook, because he knew that many students probably didn't read it, and he suspected that many of them probably didn't even buy it. However, all of his students had seen his notes as he had presented them in class and then the examples that he had made that explained the material to them.

He started leafing through his course notes.

Over the years he had found that it was efficient to summarize textbook material on 3 x 5 note papers to remind him of the topics that he would like to cover in each class. To these, he added examples from his own working experiences, as well as points that he had made from current articles. He had a set of these notes for each of the courses that he taught. Some of the notes were literally falling apart from the sweat in his hands as he had held them for reference during his classes.

As he went through his notes, he was able to identify the key points that he would like to make the definition questions for. These reminded him of other questions where he could ask the students to explain the differences between different concepts instead of just defining what they were.

He went through his notes a second time to find lists of methods that he had given to the students. From these, he made up his concept questions asking for three relevant items to be listed. He was also able to take some of the methods, that had many examples associated with them, and to then make up some calculation questions for them.

One of his class presentations had been quite extensive. He made up a similar situation with a question to draw a diagram that would explain the processes that were described. Then he made up another question asking for the ways to solve the problem that was in the situation.

When he conducted his online classes, he also liked to get his students in them to summarize their learning experiences at the end of each week. He would ask them in the chat rooms:

'Name any three things that you learned this week.'

'Why are they important to you?'

'How do they impact the working environments in businesses?'

He sometimes did this in his campus courses as well.

Now that his midterm questions for next week were complete, he had to decide how many points to assign to each question. He wanted to assign fewer points to the definition questions because he knew that the students would probably just copy them from their cheat sheets. He would assign more points to the diagram question, and to the last question, because they would require more thought and creativity from the students. He distributed the remaining points to the other questions.

'I think that I'll need a second opinion on this exam on how I've constructed it,' he thought.

The first person that came to his mind was Cindy. She would have some new ideas and her university always did things a little differently. Plus he enjoyed her company and their conversations.

It took him a few tries to reach her. She did not answer her mobile phone or her home phone. It was the weekend but he decided to try her office phone at her university anyway.

"Hi, this is Cindy speaking."

"Hi, it's Mark. How is everything going? I didn't expect to find you over at the university."

"Well, since we met at the mall and then you helped me with the new software, my university decided to go back to the original software that they had. Whatever! But hey, the reason that I'm over here is to refer to my books while making up my tests for next week."

"It's interesting that you should bring up that point. I was just calling you to discuss it. My thoughts are to just use my class notes to make up my tests. I'm at home doing that right now and I just wanted to get your opinion on what I've created."

"Can I come over to look at what you've done? It would be easier than discussing it over the phone," she replied rather quickly, or so Mark thought.

"Well sure. That would be fantastic. I should have the place cleaned up by the time that you get over here."

"Your home is always spotless Mark. I'll see you shortly."

Mark scurried around tidying up a bit. Cindy was right. He did try to keep his home well organized. He then took out some finger foods that he could warm up and some other snacks.

When Cindy arrived he took her coat and then seated her in the rear family room. It had a great view out onto a treed park that was behind his home. There was a small meandering creek that ran through the middle of the park. A number of park benches were distributed throughout the area, along with picnic areas that had wood burning fire pits for family gatherings in the evenings. Several arched bridges could be seen crossing over the creek.

He already had a multi-level back deck that ran along the full width of his house to overlook the park. Soon he would be installing a sun room on half of it with a hot tub inside it. Then he could spend more time on the weekends relaxing with a few of his friends and admiring the view. He wished that he had his hot tub installed already.

"It's good to see you again Mark."

"It's also good to see you. How do you think your students have done this term?"

"Most of them are doing well. I'm worried about a couple of them. How are your students handling your course? I heard that it's quite a difficult course."

"I was worried for a while but after the review last week they all seem to be grasping the material now."

"I also do reviews with my students and that seems to help them to understand everything better. You said that you had a test that you wanted me to look over?"

Mark gave her the midterm exam that he had just made and gave her a few minutes to look at it. She asked him, "Can I see the official textbook for your course?"

He shyly watched her as she flipped through it and as she referred back to his test questions.

"There seems to be a lot of material in the textbook that is not even on your test. Why is that?"

"You know that I worked for several years as a consultant to many businesses around the world. I only want to test the students on material that they'll need to know when they start working."

Cindy pondered this for a while. He could see that she was about to say something but then she paused.

She brought her hand up to her chin, and then she said to him, "That's quite a different view from other instructors. My colleagues always test their students on everything that they can find in the course textbook. There's a lot of theory in their tests. I can see that most of yours is made up of questions that ask the students to apply their knowledge to actual business situations."

Mark appreciated her viewpoint but he felt that he had to explain his thoughts to her.

"I think that's because my educational training was rather strict at times, and I only want to focus on teaching material that the students can actually make use of later in life. My work times were also quite stressful as I worked on a number of large projects. Those projects have allowed me to bring in practical examples to the classroom to discuss with the students."

Cindy could see his viewpoint but she was curious. "I would love to hear more about those projects. But how do you accommodate all of the theory that's listed in the course outlines?"

"I still present it to the students but then I expand on it and on how to apply it to solve actual business problems. This takes me more time to prepare my courses than simply teaching using the examples in the textbook, but I feel that it is more beneficial for the students. I then focus my tests on the practical side of my courses."

"I can see what you are doing now. I'll have to try it in my own courses. You have so much more experience than me in so many things. Do you have some time now to discuss those large projects that you've worked on?"

They spent a few hours discussing his past projects, his educational experiences, and his other experiences in life.

Mark explained how he had first grown intrigued by the industrial processes that he had seen on a visit to China, while he was still in university. That had motivated him to learn more about current business and technological processes as soon as he had come back.

Later, he had worked with manufacturers to schedule the production of their goods, and then with a variety of transportation companies around the world for moving goods on land, on sea, and by air. These experiences had led to work on retail systems to sell those goods, and then to work on banking and insurance systems, in order to manage the financing for them.

His MBA studies had been taken to understand how all of these processes worked in more detail in the global economy. His PhD studies had enabled him to do research on the different technologies that were involved, and to measure the effectiveness of each technology.

Both his studies and his consulting work had also allowed him to do a fair amount of traveling to other cities, in both this country, and in other countries.

While he was talking, Cindy managed to finish all of the snacks and finger foods that he had provided for her. As the night wore on he got to know more about Cindy's experiences as well. It was well after midnight before he walked her to his door and turned in for the night.

Before he went to sleep he thought back on the projects that had helped to shape his life. Mark's last thoughts before he drifted off were of his time with Cindy that evening.

Chapter 8: Past Projects

I hear and I forget, I see and I remember, I do and I understand.
(Confucius)

One of the first projects that Mark worked on was in high school for his science fair entry. He had read a lot of material at that time about magnetic properties and electronics. He decided that he could make a small levitating saucer. He figured that a mouse could fit into it.

After he built a prototype for it, he obtained a pet mouse from a friend, put it in the saucer, and went over to his father's shop to test the saucer. He plugged it into the shop's power, turned it on, and then all hell broke loose.

His saucer did float but then every power circuit in the shop blew out with loud snapping noises, due to short circuits within the magnetic generator for the saucer. The saucer crashed to the floor, the mouse jumped out of the wreckage squealing and scurrying away, and then smoke began issuing from wiring around the shop.

The next thing that he knew, he heard sirens blaring and the fire department was on site to check out his father's shop. Later, he did perfect his levitating saucer and even won first place for it in the school's science fair. He never did see his friend's pet mouse again. But he was warned to stay away from all other projects until after he had graduated from both school, and from university. That incident also encouraged him to start working with software systems instead of hardware systems.

He was fortunate that he eventually joined a consulting company when he graduated from university. They had contracts with manufacturers, transportation companies, and several retailers. They were only a local company with a few dozen employees but they had built up an excellent reputation over the years, and they also provided services to businesses in other cities as well.

One of Mark's first jobs was to determine how all of the systems worked at a small manufacturing company that produced hundreds of motorized products. His consulting company had just acquired them as a client. The manufacturer had had several consultants and employees over the years but none of them had documented how the systems worked. The systems had been added to over time. Now the manufacturer needed to understand how everything worked so that they could enhance them for new business operations.

Mark was given the summer to figure out how everything worked. At the end of that time he would pass on his diagrams that detailed their current operations to the more senior consultants in his company. They would then use them to incorporate some new operations into the client's systems.

That job would form the foundation of Mark's skills.

He would get to see how computer systems and business systems worked together in the real world. The systems were already fully developed at the manufacturer, and so he would be able to trace information as it flowed through the various business departments and computer systems. It would also give him a chance to talk with all levels of operations staff in the company, as well as with their managers and the executives of the company.

Mark determined that he would first need some really good suits if he was going to be talking to upper management. He had never worn a suit in his life. He wanted to make a good first impression. He spent that evening visiting some men's wear stores in his area. Several suits were suggested to him. He bought a few that he liked that he could afford. He also acquired a few cool looking ties that would go along with his new suits.

After he got settled into his office at the consulting company, he headed out later that week to go over to the manufacturer. The sound of grinding and pounding machinery filled the air. His first meeting was with the president of the company.

"Greetings, Mark. Welcome to our company. I hope that you can help us out."

"I am sure that I can. I also have the entire team back at the office that I can call on if I encounter anything really complex."

"You might just be doing that. Our systems were developed by many people over the years. They have served us well so far."

After an hour spent discussing their operations with the president of the company, Mark decided that he would start by looking at their database systems. Everything fed data into them and he needed to understand how all of this data was connected between the different departments in the company. He would need to install some software tools on their systems that would help him to draw the necessary diagrams. These diagrams would then allow him to see the details of the data and the relationships between them.

He discovered that there were several groups of data that didn't seem to go anywhere. The data went in but it was never sent to the other departments, and he could not find any reports that used it. He visited the manager of the department that was collecting this data, in order to get some clarification.

"Good afternoon, Mr. Smith. I found this data in your system that no one seems to look at. Can you please explain it to me so that I can incorporate it into my documentation of your system? I would really appreciate it."

"Oh, that data! I'd completely forgotten about it. We were told a few years ago to begin collecting it for all new contracts but I guess no one thought about who would use it. I'll have to mention it to the president to see what he wants to do about it."

Mark thought, '*I wonder how many other parts of their system that I'll discover that people have forgotten about.*'

He thanked the manager and decided that he would talk to the other managers to determine what reports that they also used. He could then trace these to the data that they came from in the database.

He was starting to get a better idea of how the various systems worked. After he finished looking at the reports that were used, he then looked further into the system. He found several more reports that were in it that none of the managers had mentioned. It was time to meet with the president again.

"Good morning, sir. I hope that your week has gone well so far. Can you take a look at these reports that I found in your system? None of your managers mentioned them to me. Are they used by yourself, or perhaps by the company's auditors?"

"We used to use those reports. But that was years ago. The managers that used them left, and then the new managers had another set of reports built for them. I didn't realize that those old reports were still in the system. You can put in your documentation that they should be removed. They could be a security risk if someone else found them."

This surprised Mark. It hadn't taken him a lot of effort to find those reports in the system. Anyone working in the company could probably find them as well if they looked hard enough.

Next, he decided that he would have to talk to every clerk, accountant, shipper, and receiver at the company. He needed to find out what business forms they were putting into the system. This would take him some time to do. Then he could trace all of the input forms to the appropriate data in the database to understand where it all went to.

It was time to leave his suits at home, roll up his sleeves, and try to fit in. He had grown up in a business, and so he was quite comfortable with many of the operations that existed in a large business.

The next day, he entered the main work area of the manufacturer, grabbed a steaming hot cup of freshly brewed coffee, and walked over to a desk that they had assigned to him. He noticed that everyone was staring at him. He found out later that coffee and food was only allowed in the meeting rooms or in the lunch room. He was surprised that the coffee police hadn't come over at that time to take his coffee away from him.

While he was collecting business forms from the staff, he noticed that copies were often passed to other departments, and that the data on them was entered into the system again. He wondered, '*Why couldn't they just enter the information once, and then that data would get passed by their system into all of the related systems that needed it?*' In later years, he began to incorporate this feature into any system that he designed.

By the end of the summer, he had built up an extensive document with diagrams detailing how the current systems worked in the manufacturer, along with several recommendations on improvements that could be made.

The owner of the consulting company was impressed by his analysis and then asked him if he would mind heading up to a city in the northern part of the country.

A small airline with a dozen twin engine turboprop planes had started up there two years ago. They were currently using paper forms for all of their operations. The owner knew the president of that airline company and he had managed to get the contract to put in computer systems for them. He wanted Mark to do an analysis of their business operations, exactly like he had just completed for the manufacturer.

Mark loved flying!

Some of his uncles had small airplanes that they used to check out their farms, and he often went up with them. They would even let him take the controls once they had taken off. One day he wanted to get his own pilot's license, for both airplanes and for helicopters.

This job would be a little bit more involved than the one that he had just completed. He would also have to design the database systems once he understood how all of the operations worked, and the data that would need to be put into the system.

When Mark went up to the northern city he was greeted with a snow blizzard. He was quickly chilled to his bones from all of the ice crystals that were blowing around. What a contrast from the sunny weather that he had enjoyed on his last consulting contract!

The company had put him up at a hotel near the airport so that he could easily get to and from the airline that he would be working with. His room in the hotel overlooked the airport. He enjoyed the view that but not the pungent smell of diesel fuel that assaulted him when he opened the windows.

The next day, the airline wanted him to first understand their ticketing process.

They asked him, "Would you mind flying around with our pilots for a few days to understand our routes and the documents that we use?"

This was like a dream for him. He said, "I think that I can work that into my schedule."

He got to sit with the pilots on many of the flights and had long chats with them. He visited the agents at each location to see what information they were putting on the tickets. He also interviewed the staff at the head office to see how they were processing the tickets.

After another month, he had a pretty good idea on what was needed in a database for processing airline tickets. He even asked the airline people if he could go on some other flights, in order to clarify the details on the forms that he had collected. Some thought that he was just doing that to get joy rides, but they complied with his requests.

Mark went back to the consulting company that he worked for and spent three weeks creating a detailed design for the database that would be needed, for the input programs that would be needed for the various forms, and for the reports that would be required by the managers. His design was considered a success, and the senior consultants were able to easily use it to construct a system for the airline.

He spent the remainder of that year helping out with systems at other manufacturing companies. He also got to understand financial systems very well. These included general ledgers, receivables, payables, payrolls, and fixed asset systems.

Some of his business and computer studies at university were proving to be quite useful, as was his knowledge of operations from his father's large business.

Looking back, he realized that he should have dropped some of his university courses, and taken other courses that would have been even more useful now.

The next major client that he got involved with was a national trucking company that operated thousands of trucks. They had their head office in his city and so his company was supporting them. He heard that the company had started small with only local deliveries. Then they had expanded over the years to include other cities throughout the country.

Mark was sent over there to meet with the manager who was responsible for directing the loading of all of their trucks with deliveries. The revving of truck engines surrounded him until he could get into the quiet of the manager's office.

"I am glad that you are here Mark. Do you know anything about how we load trucks?"

"All I know is from what I have seen when my father receives shipments of cars, parts, and farm equipment. The drivers have reports that show their deliveries to each location."

"Did you ever think about how those reports were made up?"

"I just assumed that they stuffed as many items into each truck as they could, printed out a report of everything in the truck, and then sent the drivers on their way."

"It is not that easy. We have to make sure that we organize the deliveries so that the latest shipments are put in first, and that the deliveries for the first place that the drivers stop at will be put in the back of the truck. We also need to look at a map to determine the order in which we put in the shipments."

"It still sounds fairly easy."

"This is where the complications start to come in. Governments control how heavy each truck can become so that the roads don't get damaged. Packages come in different sizes and a truck can only hold so much. We make different profits depending on what is being shipped, its size, and its weight. So we must try to balance the size and weight issues to make each shipment as efficient as possible, while also trying to maximize our profits."

"How in the world do you do all of that?"

"Look at that wall in the next office. It is full of sticky papers that identify package destinations, sizes, weights, and profits. I keep moving them around until I get what I think is the best combination of deliveries for each truck.

"I think that a computer system could look at all of this, and then do a better job of scheduling our deliveries to maximize our profits. What do you think?"

Mark thought about this for a while. He realized that this could also be useful to other transportation companies, if he could figure it all out.

"I am confident that it can be done. I can create a database to hold package details, truck details, and delivery schedules. I will also need to obtain the map details on all of the cities so that the system will know how to order the deliveries.

"The hard part will be to have the computer keep rearranging the packages into truck shipments, until it gets to the maximum profit for all of them, in the minimum number of shipments."

Mark spent a couple of weeks designing, building, and testing a scheduling system. When he showed it to the trucking manager, they tried some previous weeks in it and it was always able to create more profitable schedules. The manager had just completed his suggestions for this week's shipments and so they put those into the system as well. It was able to find a 20 % improvement in profits by rearranging some packages to use fewer shipments. The manager was overjoyed!

Mark went on to consult with other transportation companies over the next year, before he turned his attention to retail companies.

The first thing that he noticed was that they had difficulties scheduling all of their part time staff. He was visiting the head offices of one of the companies to meet with their managers. They had sticky papers on their walls representing the details for their people that they had to keep moving around. They had to try to balance the skills of the people, the times and days when they were available, and their pay, in order to stay within their budgets.

This looks exactly like the transportation scheduling problem that I worked on a year ago, Mark thought.

While he was looking at the sticky papers on the office wall, he accidently knocked some of them down when he turned towards a noise in the hallway. Seeing some managers approaching, he rapidly stuck the papers back on the wall to fill in the holes in the schedules.

I hope that I put those back in the right place, or some people will have a nasty surprise in the next week when they learn about how they have been scheduled, he nervously thought.

When the retail managers stepped into the office, he quickly suggested to them that they should automate their staff scheduling. He explained what he had done before with the transportation companies. They were eager to try it out, and it took him another couple of weeks to modify his previous system, and to attach it to their payroll systems.

It worked like a charm!

While he was working with retail operations over the next few years, he also learned about inventory systems, ordering systems, and sales forecasting systems. It was very rewarding work, although there were some challenges along the way with tight deadlines and new technologies.

He was given a lot more systems to design when he joined an international consulting company. They eventually sent him to businesses in other countries where he started to learn about insurance companies, small banks, oil companies, train scheduling, and cross-border customs requirements.

The international consulting company was in another city that was half way across the country. Mark loaded up his car, and a trailer that he had rented, in order to drive to the new city. He was awed when he first saw the city. It was home to the head offices of several companies in the country.

There were high rise buildings everywhere that he looked, and construction was going on in every corner of the city. It looked like an infestation of large metallic cranes. He passed several shopping malls on his way to the apartment that he had rented. It was not until a few months later that he bought the home that he is still living in.

The first project that the new company asked him to work on was for a sales forecasting system. Their client had a huge problem with trying to predict future sales. The result was that they often bought too much inventory, or they bought too little inventory and ended up with empty store shelves. This was affecting their sales and their financing costs.

Mark worked together with a team to develop methods that looked at several years of sales data to find patterns that were occurring from season to season. They were successful in obtaining accurate predictions for buying inventory and so they automated the entire process for the client.

Mark went on to develop other systems, in coordination with other teams from around the world.

One of the more interesting projects that he was asked to work on was to create an artificially intelligent computer system to replace all of the parts people in a national vehicle service operation. They had service centers in hundreds of locations across the country. They had always found it a challenge to find people that knew the details of the vehicles for all manufacturers, for all years, for the parts that would fit them, and for the parts that would be needed for each type of service request.

"You want to do what?" exclaimed Mark, upon arriving at a meeting that had been set up by their corporate executives.

"Let me start by explaining how our current operation works. Then you can see where the challenges are."

"I am all ears."

"When a customer arrives with their vehicle, we start by asking for the year of the vehicle, the make, the model, the size of the engine, the type of transmission, and whether it has air conditioning installed. Some customers don't know this, and so we have to get a technician to first look it over. This takes time."

"Wait. Didn't you know that you can get all of that information from the vehicle identification number that is on their registration papers?" said Mark. The training that he had received in his early years in his father's business was proving to be extremely useful right now.

"Really? What do you suggest?"

"For starters, I can set up an interface to the registry databases, so that once you enter the number in the system, then you will be able to see all of the relevant data on the vehicle."

"That would be great! However, that is the easy part. We are just getting started with explaining what happens next. We then ask the customer what service they would like. This could be a minor tune up, major tune up, brake job, or any of a variety of service requests. I will let Paul explain what happens next at this point."

"We now pass on all of this information to a parts expert. They use their knowledge of how various vehicles are manufactured, in order to come up with a list of the parts that are needed.

"They then determine if we have those parts, or compatible parts, in our inventory. When we don't have the parts then the parts will have to be ordered in from the dealers. As a final step, our parts experts will schedule the work through our service bays, using their knowledge of the order in which the jobs must be done, and of who has the skills to do those jobs."

Mark could be seen furiously taking down notes, and scribbling ideas on the side.

"And you want me to put the brains and experience of your parts people into a computer system?" he said, in amazement.

"If I were to sum all of this up in a nutshell, then yes! What do you think?"

Mark was thinking of many things. Most of them were not repeatable to the executives.

He finally said, "Leave it with me for a few days. I will get back to you."

Everyone told him that this project was impossible to do. They said that many people had already tried and failed. Mark didn't believe in the words 'it cannot be done.' He believed that there was always a way once you set your mind to it. To him, a problem was just a solution in disguise.

He spent some time examining the client's current paperwork and their work schedules. Next, he looked at the databases that were available to them. He even called up his father to find out how he ran his service operations.

Finally, he searched for current material on how artificially intelligent systems used neural networks to make decisions. He eventually came up with a basic design. He met with the executives again to discuss his ideas.

"You will be delighted to know that what you want can be done. I have also determined that you will get several other benefits from this system."

"This was exactly what we wanted to hear. Please explain how the system will work and what you will need from us."

"By using your payroll system, I can access the work schedules of all of your technicians. But I will need you to input all of their skills into a new database that I will create. That will allow the system to assign jobs to the technicians as the service requests come in."

"We can do that," one of the executives readily agreed.

"Next, I noticed that you have the parts manuals for all of the vehicles that you service. You need to contact the manufacturers to get licenses for database access to the details in those manuals. This will allow the system to search through the databases to find the parts that it needs."

"This will take us a little longer to arrange but it is still doable," another executive said.

"Finally, I will need you to input the names of every type of service that you offer to your customers, the time required to do those services, the skills required to do those services, and the names of the parts that are needed for them. I will create a new database for you to use. The names of the parts can be as simple as pad, caliper, plug, and so forth.

"The new computer system will then use those names to search the appropriate manufacturer databases to find the exact parts. When it cannot find the parts in your inventory then it will also place electronic orders to the appropriate dealers to obtain them."

"We can definitely ask our technicians for help in determining what is needed for each service. What else?"

Mark paused for a moment to gather his thoughts.

"Now comes the hard part. I will need to create a program that will use all of this information to determine the parts to use for service requests, the technicians to use, and the order in which to schedule the jobs in your service bays. I need to be careful that I don't schedule anyone to work on two jobs at the same time."

"You had mentioned that the system will give us other benefits. What are those?"

"Because the system is scheduling the technicians itself, it will be able to pass on the jobs assigned to them directly into your payroll systems. This will eliminate all of the paperwork for recording those details.

"Also, because the system knows the time to do all of the jobs, the technicians that are available each day, and it knows what jobs that it has scheduled, it will be able tell you when the next available time is for servicing any new customer request."

"That is fantastic!" all of the executives said at once.

It took Mark and the executive team a few months to get all of the programs and databases working properly. The intelligent system was installed in all of their service locations, and was a great boon to their business. As word of this system got around, Mark was soon inundated with requests to design other advanced systems for clients.

In later years, he even managed to publish a few articles on using electronic commerce in businesses. Later he did research that compared the different types of technology that could be used to build systems for businesses.

'*The universities should teach all of this stuff that I have been learning,*' Mark thought.

Chapter 9: The Test

Is there a person who has not made one error and half a mistake? (Lao Tzu)

The night before Mark's midterm exam was to begin it had started to pour rain. Numerous lightning flashes lit up the night sky along with thunderous booms. The next morning it was still raining heavily.

Mark thought, '*I hope that all of my students are able to show up today for the test that I designed this weekend. The city sometimes closes roads when it rains this much.*'

He found that the traffic was very congested as he headed out, and he had to endure several long waits. He tried other routes but it was the same. He was worried that he would be late for his exam.

In frustration, he decided to head out of the city to go past the airport by using the country roads. Then he could head back into the city to get to the university that was on the edge of it. This would increase his travel time but he figured that he should just be able to make it to the university before the exam.

He saw flooding everywhere that he looked and many roads were impassable. Shortly after passing the airport, he realized that this route had also become impassable. He would not be able to use it to return to the city. Therefore, he turned around and headed back to the airport to look for their heliport.

"Hi. Can I rent or charter one of your helicopters to get over to the university?" he asked.

"Sorry. All of our helicopters are currently out helping with the flooding emergency," he was told.

"How about those owned by private individuals? I can see them parked over there."

"None of those owners are here this early in the morning. Wait! One of our helicopters is coming in now. Our owner is in it and you can discuss your needs with him."

Mark glanced anxiously at his watch. He thought, '*I may have to call the university and cancel my exam if I can't work out something in the next few minutes.*' When he saw the owner walking over to the hangar office, he approached him.

"Excuse me. I am a pilot but I am also a university professor. This rain has made the roads impassable and I am scheduled to give an exam at the university this morning. Is there any chance that we can work something out to get me over there?"

"This is your lucky day. I'm passing within a few blocks of it on my next flight and I can drop you off. Don't worry about any fees. The city is paying for my time to help them out with this emergency. Let's head over there right now."

Mark couldn't believe it! He had been prepared to pay for the time to airlift him to the university. It would have been a short journey but he had felt a responsibility to show up for his exam on time.

Once they were in the air, he could see flooding throughout the city. Most of the roads were closed, with cars either parked on the sides or floating in the middle of them. It looked like pure chaos. He was worried about his students who lived off campus who would be trying to get to the university.

He was surprised that the university had not put out an announcement that the classes were cancelled. He could easily have rescheduled his exam.

While they were flying in the helicopter, Mark was careful not to distract the pilot. He knew from his own flying how sensitive helicopters were to small adjustments on their controls. He also knew that all of the control adjustments had to be precisely controlled in order to have a stable flight in a helicopter.

He could remember when he had first started learning to fly helicopters. He thought that he could just move the cyclic control stick forward to start flying forward. But that resulted in the helicopter also losing lifting power from the angle of the blades. So he had to pull up on the collective control to maintain his height from the ground. This then resulted in more effort for the blades to rotate through the air and they started slowing down and causing him to lose height again. He would rotate the collective control to give them more power from the engine but then a new problem would show up.

The helicopter would start to rotate from the increased power being given to the blades. So now he had to use his foot pedals to adjust the power that was going to the tail rotor so that the helicopter kept flying straight. It seemed that every time he made a turn, adjusted his height, or encountered some wind, he had to try to balance out all of the other forces that were acting on the helicopter. It had taken him some time before he had mastered his control of a helicopter.

Shortly after he had gone up in this current helicopter, the pilot successfully maneuvered it to touch down on a vacant corner of the university's grounds. Mark shook hands with the pilot before opening the door to exit the aircraft. Some of the students at the university recognized him when he was getting out of the helicopter. They immediately rushed over to him.

"Jeez, Professor! How come you get to ride in a helicopter over here, and we have to drive over or take the bus?"

Mark just smiled.

Upon arriving at his classroom, he noticed that most of his students were already there. He knew that many of them lived in residence at the university. He would need to make up an alternative exam for any students that could not make it in due to the flooding.

One of his students was making a racket by pulling out a huge rustling piece of crumpled flipchart paper that was two feet by three feet in size. Upon walking over to him, he said, "Edward, what in the world is that?"

"You said that we could write notes on one piece of paper. You didn't say how big the paper could be."

"Look around you Edward. Everyone has papers that are the same size as their notebooks."

Edward pulled out a regular sized paper from his backpack and asked, "Like this?"

"That is better."

"I just wanted to see what I could get away with. Remember that I did say to you in the computer conference on the weekend that you'd owe me a favor, for carrying all of the vendor brochures and their gifts for you."

"I was just thinking about paying for your lunch one day at the university."

Mark exhaled in exasperation.

As he was walking back to his desk, a student rushed past him. He felt something brush up against his legs as well. Looking down, he saw a wet dog with drooping ears looking up at him.

"Well hello there. Where did you come from?"

The student who had just come in turned to him and said, "That's Charlie. He's stressing out with all of this rain and so I brought him with me. Don't worry. He'll sit quietly at the front of the class. He's a nice dog."

Mark had never heard of anything like this in his entire life. He was not even sure of what the university regulations were for it. The dog continued to look at him while dripping all over the carpet in the classroom.

"The exam starts in a couple of minutes. I will allow it for now but if he makes a fuss then I will have to call security to bring him outside."

"Let him stay Professor," some of the other students said.

When he was passing out the exam papers Mark also tried to give one to the dog just for fun. The dog promptly took a bite out of it and then set it aside. Mark's students looked surprised.

"I guess there is a critic in every class," he said.

The students got a good laugh out of it, and then put their heads down to work on their midterm exam.

Mark's exam was scheduled for three hours but one student handed it in after less than 30 minutes. When he flipped through it quickly he noticed that several answers had been left blank. He was sure that students who left early probably knew the answers to the questions shortly after leaving the exam room, when they had time to calm down.

He wished that students would spend the full time thinking about their answers. He didn't understand their desire to rush out of their exams as quick as they could. Exams represented a major portion of their course marks and he thought that they should be more careful with their answers.

About an hour later, two students put up their hands. He walked over to them and one student asked him to clarify the situation that needed a diagram. He pointed out some things that should be considered since the student would still have to figure out how to draw the diagram on her own. The other student asked him for the meaning of one of the definition questions.

"I won't be able to help you on that one. Those are definition questions and if I tell you the meaning then you will know the answer."

He saw a student in the back of the room that seemed to be glancing at the papers on the left and right sides of him. When he went over there to challenge the student, Mark was told by the student that he was just stretching his neck. "Then stretch it forward only. This is an individual exam and not a group exam," he reminded the student.

He could recall that the university used to provide exam assistants to help with answering questions, and with monitoring student activities during exams. There even used to be hall monitors who would go with the students when they had to step out for a few minutes. However, budgetary constraints at the university had caused them to drop all of the assistants several years ago. Now instructors were expected to monitor all of the exam activities by themselves.

The dog at the front of the room was watching him intently as he wandered among the students to check on how they were doing.

When he passed by the dog, he asked him, "I suppose that you have a question too?"

The dog just gave him a couple of guttural barks but Mark couldn't figure out what he was asking.

The rest of the exam was going smoothly. Some other students started to finish their papers and to hand them in. Most of them patted or played with the dog for a while before leaving the classroom.

About half way through the exam, a student rushed in out of breath.

"Sorry sir. I got tied up in the traffic getting here. Can I still write the exam?"

"You can but it is half over. Do you want to do it in the remaining time, or would you feel better writing the alternative exam this Friday?"

"I know the material really well. I just want to get it done. Hey, why is there a dog in the classroom?" he exclaimed when the dog came over and started sniffing him.

"Oh him! He got permission from the university to challenge this exam."

The student just gave him a puzzled look and then sat down to write the exam.

All was going well for the next few minutes until Edward decided to sharpen a few pencils. The electric machine that he was using was making so much whining noise that Mark had to rush over to tear it away from him.

"Here is a pen, Edward," he said. There was silent applause from those students that were still trying to write the exam. Edward managed to finish up his exam 30 minutes later and then he left, after silently saying *sorry* to everyone.

Over the next hour, most of the students finished their exams and handed them in. A few of them had dazed looks on their faces. Mark wondered if he had looked like them when he had written his undergraduate exams.

Finally, by the end of the exam time, there were only three students left in the room.

"There are only 10 minutes left," Mark reminded them.

One of the students was the one that had come in late. Another was the student who had brought in the dog. The third student was Marcia. This surprised Mark as she was fairly bright, and he was not sure why she needed to stay so late to work through the exam questions.

The first two students finished their exam papers in the next few minutes. As the student with the dog was leaving, he said, "Thank you for allowing Charlie to be here during the exam."

"It was a pleasure to have him here. And I think that all of the other students appreciated him as well. I love animals."

Marcia glanced up when Mark said that, and smiled, but then she went back to working on her paper.

When the clock's buzzer sounded, Mark announced, "Time's up. Please hand in your exam paper Marcia."

"Here it is, sir. I also put some comments in it to explain my answers, and to ask you some questions."

Mark thought, '*I wonder what she could possibly want to ask me? Maybe she wants to do some extra studying like I used to do, and she just needs some advice on what to study?*'

Marcia smiled at him as she left and he smiled back.

Before he gathered up his exam papers, he checked the room for any items that the students might have left behind. He discovered a phone that someone had left charging in a corner, as well as a coat on one of the chairs. He took these over to the lost and found department at the university and then headed back to his office in another building by cutting through some other buildings.

He could see that it was still pouring rain outside. The students could be seen dashing between the buildings while trying to avoid it. Many of them were holding up their backpacks above their head.

Mark wanted to first make up an alternative exam for Friday, for those students who had missed the exam today. He could not just give them the same exam, because he knew that some of them might ask their classmates what the questions were on the test.

He started by finding other definitions in his notes to replace those in the exam. Then he changed the business situation that was described so that the students would have to draw a different type of diagram for it, and so that they would have to come up with a different solution for it. For the calculation questions, he just changed the numbers that were in the question. It took him a little longer to find alternatives for the other questions in the exam, but he was finally done rewriting the exam an hour later.

He planned to do the marking for all of the exams on the weekend when he could focus on them for a few hours. He always liked to carefully consider the answers that were given on each exam, and to add comments to explain any marks that were taken away.

He could remember getting back a paper one time in his doctoral studies that just got a 95, but there were no comments in the paper to explain why the marks were lost. His next paper got an 85, again with no comments in it. When he had asked his professor why the marks were lost, he was told that his paper had felt like an 85. He had found that totally unacceptable in an educational environment.

He felt that students deserved to be told exactly why marks were lost so that they could improve future papers when they turned them in, and also so that they would know what material they needed to review.

He also felt that they should get back all of their tests and assignments within a week, so that they were not left in the dark wondering what grades they had received on their work.

This weekend would be a busy one for him at home and he looked forward to seeing the answers that the students gave, and any comments that they had put into their exam papers. He thought back on his own schooling and on the times when he had had others to share his life with.

Chapter 10: Home Life

The will to win, the desire to succeed, the urge to reach your full potential... These are the keys that will unlock the door to personal excellence. (Confucius)

The schools in Mark's childhood did not just pass students into the next grade. Teachers were allowed to give failing grades in classes when work was not done, or when work showed minimal effort. Students learned to study hard, or to be left behind. Mark had known a few who had had to repeat grades. He did notice that those students who had repeated courses to get better grades in them were better prepared when they eventually went on to either college or university.

He found the subjects in school fascinating, and he could not understand why others were challenged by them. For sure, there were some subjects, such as the sciences, where he did better than in other subjects, such as the arts. But the teachers were always there, and they were always willing to help.

The core courses were planned out for all students. Optional courses were offered for other subjects that might interest the students. In later years, there were also advanced levels offered for all of the courses for those students who were planning to go to university.

There was enough time given between classes for students to work on their homework. Mark took full advantage of this time, in order to complete all of his assignments before he left school.

He wanted time later on to explore the school library, as well as the town library. It seemed to him that there was so much to learn and that the world offered so much. Then, on weekends, when he wasn't asked to help out on one of his uncles' farms, he would explore the countryside around his home.

Mark was raised in a traditional family. His mom stayed at home and took care of the house, along with him and his younger brother and sisters. He could remember how the captivating scent of fresh baking often filled the house. His father focused on his current work, as well as on building up his business. He always made time to come back home for lunch, and to return home for supper each evening.

He had told Mark that family must always come before work in the evenings. His thoughts were that you got to see your family once but that work would always be there. Mark never saw his father go back to work at night. He would spend time at home chatting with the family, or working on projects around the house.

He also worked on Saturdays but then he always took time off on Sundays, in order to take the family to visit relatives. He had a tradition of holding barbeques every Sunday. Many relatives and friends would come over for those events.

Mark could recall one time when his father had asked his mother to get the barbeque started, while he went to the store to pick up some more steaks. His mother managed to get a corner of their house burning, as well as the barbeque.

"Quick, Mark, call the fire department," his mother screamed, while trying to frantically beat out the fire with a blanket that was nearby.

When the firemen arrived, Mark's dog would not let them into the house. Mark had to be sent back into the burning house to drag out his growling dog. By the time that his father arrived back at the house, the fire was out and everyone was just sitting around talking about it. Needless to say, his mother was never allowed to start the barbeque again!

That was when his father decided that he needed a new house. He found a spot about a mile outside of the town that they were living in. It was on a hill, surrounded by a few trees, with a small winding creek running along one side of it. It was the former site of a communications tower that had recently been moved to another location.

His father then spent the next three years building a house on the hill. He did most of the work himself but he frequently persuaded his family, and Mark's uncles, to help out as well.

It was an exciting time for Mark. He watched with interest to see how a house was built, and he helped out wherever he could.

Inspired by what he was seeing, Mark started confiscating all of the loose materials that he could find. Including some materials that he shouldn't have confiscated! It wasn't long before he had his own small house constructed in a nearby tree.

He thought that it was great, but the first storm that came through the area totally demolished his tree house! He ended up rebuilding it, and he made sure to use stronger bracing in every part of it. Over the next few years he had had tons of fun in it, and he was always adding new features to it such as a wraparound deck and shuttered windows.

His father also decided that they needed a few more trees along one side of their property, as a wind break. Over the next few days, he had had some young trees planted on the property, just before they moved into their new estate home. The next morning, all of the young trees were gone!

"Where are all of the trees?" exclaimed Mark, upon waking up.

"Who would steal trees?" his father replied.

They all rushed outside to examine the trees. The base of all of the trees had bite marks on them. There were drag marks in the ground, heading back towards the creek. They followed the trail of evidence and discovered that a family of beavers had moved in. They were happily chewing up the new trees and were using them to construct a dam across the creek.

Mark's dog made a valiant effort to chase all of them away but they skillfully avoided him. Later, his dog seemed to make peace with them, and he could often be seen in future weeks spending his time swimming with the beavers.

"I guess that we'll need a steel fence around our trees," his father said. He had a new row of trees planted and then he put up a fence around them. A few of the older trees on their property then disappeared. Eventually the beavers were all moved in and they were satisfied with the dam that they had created, and with the homes that they had built behind the dam.

His family then obtained a small lawn tractor for cutting all of the grass on the large property that their house was on. Mark instantly volunteered to drive it around to cut all of the grass. He spent most weekends cutting the grass for a couple of hours, whether the grass needed cutting or not. The lawn tractor was not very fast, and it was not a go-kart, but he still enjoyed driving it around their property.

The next excitement occurred when his mother had gotten a garden started in one corner of their property. A few weeks later, a deer could be seen wandering through her garden eating all of the young sprouts. Other deer could be seen standing around near the edge of the garden. It didn't take long before his family put up another steel fence around the garden area.

Around this time, his father also constructed an enclosed gazebo at another corner of the property. It had large windows looking out onto the creek and onto the surrounding countryside. Mark often spent time in it admiring the tranquil view, while he was busy studying the books that he had brought back from the town library.

His grandfather was also skilled in woodcraft and he was always making a variety of three dimensional wooden puzzles for him to solve. Some of them were quite challenging. Mark often had to resort to disassembling them in order to figure out how they worked. He frequently watched the wildlife around the area while he was trying to figure out the puzzles.

So far, he had encountered a variety of wild animals in his life. First, a raccoon had wandered into his room when he was quite young, and it had stayed with him for a few months. In primary school, he had seen a live leopard that a farmer had brought to his school.

Now he had recently seen some beavers and a family of deer. Not to mention all of the rabbits that he saw every day, and the foxes or wolves who were chasing them. One morning, he had even seen a moose down by the creek while he was reading in the gazebo. The next wild animal that he saw was a little scarier.

He had learned to ride horses at an early age. The next week, he was out riding on one of his uncles' farms checking out the fence lines. His dog, Prince, was with him. Suddenly, his horse became very skittish. Approaching them from behind some trees was a small brown bear.

"Whoa! Settle down!" he said, as he tried to calm down his horse.

"Prince! Get back here!" he shouted to his dog, which had gone after the bear.

He watched in amazement as his dog faced off against the bear. There was a lot of barking and growling but eventually the bear turned tail and then headed back into the trees. Mark had to persuade his dog to come back to him in order to continue with the ride. The rest of the day went smoothly, but Mark now found himself constantly looking around whenever he was getting near any trees.

It was not until later in the day that he saw his dog suddenly collapse. The bear had tragically scratched Prince on his lower abdomen. His dog had tried to keep up with Mark that day but his injuries had proved to be too much for him. Mark carried him home on his horse's saddle and then gently laid him to rest by a tree on their property.

After that event, his father decided to take him to a large lake that was nearby. He told him, "There is nothing in the lake that can attack you. You can just relax."

"What about lake monsters, Father?"

"They only have those in other countries," his father replied, with a serious tone and a wink.

His father had to go out and borrow a houseboat from a relative. The boat looked like a large square box that was sitting on a boat hull. Inside, it was just like a small house. It had two stories, with bedrooms, a living room, a dining room, a kitchen, and two complete washrooms.

There were railings around it, to assist with getting in and out of the water, and a sun deck on the top with lounge chairs. Mark had a quiet couple of days on the boat but he missed his dog. Prince would have loved jumping off the boat and swimming around the lake. Mark went back on houseboats at a few other times later in his life. There were lots of inlets and small villages to explore along the lake shore.

There were quite a few times when Mark was taken camping as well. He was shown how to make housing from materials in the forest, how to start fires for cooking, how to find good water, how to find non-poisonous wild fruits and vegetables, and how to do basic outdoor cooking. The cooking was not as fancy as that done by his mother, but the food from it was still quite nourishing.

His father also made him take a number of wilderness first aid courses, which were much more comprehensive than the basic first aid courses that were offered by most organizations. The wilderness courses covered the treating of poisonous bites and the setting of fractures and dislocations in the joints. Later, Mark acquired many books on wilderness medicine and everyday medical treatments so that he could discuss matters with doctors in a more informed manner.

The only thing that he found hard about his camping trips was trying to get to sleep at night. Between the chirping crickets, the buzzing insects, the hooting owls, and the yapping coyotes, he felt that it was noisier than the downtown area of a city during its rush hour.

His father had been raised when times were harsh, and he had been taught how to be self-sufficient. He felt that Mark should have those same skills.

All of this was how Mark viewed family life. He thought that all families were the same. These thoughts remained with him throughout his university studies over the next few years.

When he was introduced to his wife Evelyn in his last year at university, he thought that she would hold the same viewpoints as him. He thought that he could focus on work, and that together they could work on raising the family that he was so eager to start.

Even though his mother had never worked in businesses, Mark thought that it was great when his wife wanted to apply her skills in the workforce. And he could definitely help out with cooking and household chores, but he was not sure if his wife would appreciate his campsite style of cooking.

He was initially drawn to her by the intensity of her studying. It matched his own intense need to study as much as he could. She was already finishing up her third university degree. She had previously worked on two university degrees at the same time. One was in electrical engineering and the other was in business.

She had come from a large business family that was always pushing her to succeed. She got exemptions for many of the courses in her third degree, which was in computer science. Mark was able to help her out in her last few courses. It was true that she was slightly older than him, but it was her mind that attracted him to her when they were introduced by other students.

Their wedding had followed immediately after his graduation. Her parents were still not fond of him, since he only had one university degree, and he did not even own his own business.

On their wedding night, she asked him, "Would you mind if I went back to my country to visit my parents for a month? I'd like to try to smooth things over with them."

"That would be fine. I'll try to find some nice housing for us while you are away. I think that I'll also be busy getting started with my new job."

At the end of the month, during one of their regular conversations, she asked, "Would you mind if I stayed another two months to visit my parents?"

Mark just sighed. "I'm not crazy about this. Get back as soon as you can."

Towards the end of that time, he received a call from his excited wife, "Guess what? I got a contract for a year for a high paying job. I can use most of my skills in that job. It'll allow me to get some relevant work experience before I come back and get a job there. Isn't that great?"

Mark didn't think it was great.

He thought that married people were supposed to build a life together.

"There are lots of jobs here. I'm overloaded with work in my company."

"But they don't pay as well! I'll be designing new control equipment for the factories over here and then creating the software to monitor it. It's a great opportunity. It'll only be for a year. We can be together after that."

Mark was in tears and he was heartbroken. He had to admit that it was a great opportunity for his wife, but he wondered how he would ever get through the next year.

He ended up throwing himself into his work and into as many evening courses as he could.

From his previous studies, he had already taken courses in accounting, finance, law, taxation, project management, marketing methods, and economics to understand banking and business systems in more detail. Those courses had also helped him to manage his personal affairs better. On top of those courses, he added others that dealt with new technologies, stock market analysis, real estate investing, and house maintenance.

There was one night that the instructor did not show up for the technology course. Mark took it upon himself to teach the class that night. He showed the other students how he could use some of the new technologies in projects that he was currently working on. This gave his classmates ideas of their own. They were soon all discussing the practical applications of the course material in their own projects. Mark enjoyed passing on his experiences. This was the first time that he felt like he would want to do more teaching in the future.

He spent every weekend either working or studying. It was a hard year on him, but his wife reluctantly came back to him at the end of that time.

He was overjoyed to see her again. Her thoughts on the matter were completely different.

"You can't believe the opportunities that I had to give up to come back here. I could've been making so much money right now!"

"Don't worry Evelyn. With your skills, there will be lots of opportunities for you here. And we can be together now. It'll be great."

It turned out to be difficult for her to initially find full time employment. Everyone thought that she was over qualified for jobs. It was also true that she asked for high pay due to all of her degrees. Despite this, she was able to obtain several contracts over the years and also some part time work as well. Her specialty was in designing control software for manufacturers, and later for some oil and gas companies.

She was able to travel with Mark whenever he went on business trips, and they were able to explore many cities together. She made many contacts with businesses during those trips and she consulted with them on an ongoing basis over the next few years.

However, she made him stop taking all of his evening courses. She pushed him to take on extra work every evening and every weekend. She set up a consulting company for him so that he could do this. Whenever he wanted to take an annual vacation, she was quick to point out to him all the money that he would be losing by taking time off from work. She told him to work now while the money was good, and to only think about vacations much later in his life.

It was years later before he started taking some evening courses again to update his technological skills. The projects that he was working on were getting more complex and he needed to know about many of the new technologies in order to get the work for those projects.

Eventually it all got to be too much for him. He had an appendix attack one day at work, and this started him thinking about his life. He gave up all of his extra work, began pursuing an MBA degree to further his career, and then started spending more time on the weekends back at a lake to relax.

By the time that he had his MBA, and was started on a new career teaching in a university, Evelyn had divorced him to do consulting around the world. To his knowledge, she was still doing that.

The next lady that he met was Natalia, who was considerably younger than him. She had only one university degree in business, but she was also from a large business oriented family. Her approach to life was a lot more carefree. She had been in banking in her country, and she had initially come to this country to be with her sister.

He had met her while she was trying a course at the university where he taught. She eventually started a successful business with her sister, and later she bought out that business from her sister.

Mark helped her to set up her business with the latest computer technology in it. There was one period when several competitors had opened up businesses near to her. He noticed that she refused to lower her prices, the quality of her goods, or the quality of her services. She initially lost some customers, but most of them came back after about a year.

Her business was located on a ground floor, facing out onto a major road that was bustling with tourists. As a result of this, she got a lot of walk-in business.

The wasps in the area also seemed to like buzzing into her business and scaring away her customers. Mark read that if you blow up a brown paper sandwich bag and hang it up by a front door, then all of the wasps will stay away. Apparently, they thought that it was a hive that belonged to another colony, and so they avoided the area. Mark gave it a try and it worked!

One day, Natalia asked him, "Would you mind if my parents came to visit with us for a few months? I haven't seen them in a while. Plus they could help me out in my business during the day."

"You mean, live with us?"

"Of course! Don't be silly. That's what parents do."

Mark wondered if the paper bag trick would work on her parents.

As it turned out, her parents ended up staying for over a year. They had to have their visitor visas extended twice so that they could spend more time with their daughter. They took over all of the cooking in the household, and Mark was privileged to enjoy a different kind of meal every day.

"What is that?" he would frequently inquire at meal times.

"Don't ask. Just eat it," was the reply that was always given to him.

There was one day when he arrived home to an empty house. He immediately noticed a very strong putrid odor throughout his home. It took him awhile to track it down, but it was coming from a container in one of the kitchen cupboards. He promptly threw it out. When Natalia and her parents came back, her father was distraught because he could not find the special sauce that he had been preparing for their next meal. Mark could only thank his lucky stars that he had disposed of it, before he had to taste it on his next meal.

Natalia's parents had also picked up a variety of folk medicine treatments from around the world. They were only too happy to practice them on Mark whenever he got sick.

As soon as they noticed that he was ill, then they would brew up some kind of dark and foul smelling concoction, and then ask him to drink it. It tasted even worse than it looked but Mark had to admit that it worked. However, those treatments prompted him to try his very best to remain healthy so that he would not suffer one of their treatments. He sometimes thought that he would prefer to be ill, rather than have to drink one of their medicines.

The only medicine that Mark enjoyed from them was the one that they gave him for a cold. They would chop up fresh ginger into small pieces, and then they would throw those into a pan that was full of Coca-Cola from a can. They would get this boiling, and then immediately put it into a large cup for Mark to drink. It was very spicy but it worked like a charm!

Natalia was truly a blessing in Mark's life. She got his house organized, was with him every night and weekend, and had encouraged him to pursue a PhD degree when she had first met him. She had offered her support throughout all of his struggles with his PhD studies. Even her parents had helped out with numerous household chores so that Mark could focus on his doctoral studies.

Later, Natalia liked telling all of her friends about how she had married a professor. She even made a poem about it.

There was a person who wandered wide.
She found a professor who used to hide.
Now he is cool and can show his pride.
And give daily thanks for his lovely bride.

They spent many evenings out on Mark's back deck watching the orange glow of sunsets and their reflections on the clouds. They even managed to camp out in his backyard a few times. Luckily, there were no hooting owls or yapping coyotes by his home!

They also went on many vacations together around the world. Oftentimes, she was able to join him on a number of his business and computer conferences in other countries. Her extensive knowledge of cultures was actually able to help him through many of his dealings with students in his classrooms.

One of Natalia's hobbies was singing, and he enjoyed hearing her each morning as she refined her art. She was able to win several major competitions and eventually she had a professional recording made of her songs.

There was one summer that she became friends with a casting director for a Hollywood movie that was filming cowboy scenes in the surrounding area. She was able to get both herself and Mark into the movie as extras. She got a day on the set while Mark got a whole week on the set. Everyone had to show up at 6 AM for makeup and then they had to work until midnight.

The first morning that Mark showed up, he went looking for their food tent for some breakfast. He quickly found it near some rather large motorhomes. The food in the tent was arranged on several tables just like the buffet tables at a luxury hotel. He loaded up two plates that were overflowing with great food. All of the actors were staring at him while he was eating.

Afterwards, he wandered around and discovered a much smaller tent. It was the food tent for the extra actors. The only food that was served in it was an egg on a bun. No wonder all of the major actors had been staring at him in the main tent. They probably couldn't figure out who he was or what movies he had made.

In the first scene that day, the director yelled "Background," and no one moved. Everyone was waiting for him to shout "Action." The assistant director then had to explain to them that the extras were supposed to move as part of the background, and that the major actors would move once action was called for.

Mark found that he had to be constantly on the alert for all of the horses that were dashing around, so that he did not get trampled by them. Not to mention the stone that was thrown in one of the scenes. A lady actor was asked to throw a stone at another major actor, but she was advised not to hit him or his horse. Her large stone whizzed past Mark and took down a camera man by hitting him in his forehead. When they re-filmed the scene, Mark noticed that all of the cowboys around him were using their hats as catcher's mitts to try to catch the stone that was thrown.

It was hilarious!

Most of the scenes were about two minutes apiece, and many of them had to be filmed several times until the director felt that everything was acceptable. Lots of mistakes were always being made. In one bar scene, an extra tried to drink the fake liquor and then he promptly gagged on it. This caused all of the others in the scene to burst out laughing. When they tried to film the scene again, the major actor could not get into the bar. Someone had accidently locked the door. They could all hear him rattling it and throwing his weight against it trying to get in.

Overall, Mark had a great time making his movie debut. When the movie came out, he noticed that two of his days had been completely cut out from the movie, and that he only got about 20 seconds of fame in the middle of the movie. Natalia was luckier and she got her 20 seconds of fame in the opening scene when it started. She was wearing a red silk dress in that scene and she could be seen putting on the makeup for one of the major actresses in that movie.

Mark was devastated when he lost Natalia shortly after that. He was not sure what to do to cope with his loss. He approached the administrators at his university to see if they could give him some more responsibilities.

"We have some new evening and weekend programs starting up Mark. Do you think that you could handle them at this point in your life?"

"I need something. Anything that will take my mind off of my situation will help. Some friends have been over and they have said that work is the best cure for me right now."

"I understand. I will send the course outlines and schedules over to you. Let me know if there is anything that I, or anyone else, can do to help you out."

Mark did manage to get his life back on track but it took time.

Students became the focus of his life. He gained immense satisfaction from working with them to help them succeed in their studies.

After another year, he cut back on the number of courses that he was teaching, in order to take some courses of his own. He began taking more time for trips to lakes on the weekends to relax. He also did more personal flying to appreciate the tranquil lake and river views around his home.

He wondered what life had in store for him and what new people he would meet in the future.

Chapter 11: The Evaluation

Better a little which is well done, than a great deal imperfectly. (Plato)

When Mark sat down to grade the stack of midterm exam papers that was in front of him, he sighed. This always took him several hours to do.

The university used to provide marking assistants for the professors. Mark could remember that he used to just make up marking guides for the assistants. They would then have all of the papers graded a week later. The university paid the assistants a fee for doing this, plus the assistants considered it a privilege to be selected to do the grading for a professor. However, budgetary constraints at the university had caused them to drop all of the assistants several years ago.

Mark knew that a number of instructors had simplified their tests and assignments when this had happened, so that they could minimize the amount of time that they spent marking them. However, he continued to use his comprehensive tests and assignments because he had seen what was required by businesses when he was working with them.

He wanted his students to be fully prepared for their careers when they eventually graduated.

The university had also dropped all supervised lab times. Mark used to spend time in the labs helping students to understand the course material better. He was able to coach many students to higher marks in his courses.

Now the university expected students to just learn the material on their own. This was why Mark felt an obligation to continue to offer practical examples in his courses, in order to shorten the learning times for his students.

The first paper that he picked up was from Patrick. He was always very quiet in class, and he happened to be the student who had rushed out of the exam after only the first few minutes. When Mark looked through the paper he could see that most of the answers that were given were correct, but that the majority of the questions in the exam had been left blank. He was sure that Patrick knew the answers but he just seemed to freeze up whenever he wrote tests. Mark had to assign a failing grade to the paper but he made a note to talk to Patrick to see if he, or the university, could help him out in any way.

The next paper that he picked up was written by Tim. He had left before the exam was half over. There were answers to all of the questions but a lot of them were incorrect or partially incorrect. Mark could not understand why Tim felt the need to rush out of the exam, and why he did not spend the extra time to double check all of his work. There was enough in the exam paper that was correct that Mark was able to assign a barely passing grade to Tim's paper. But Tim could have done so much better if he had just focused on those areas that he was most comfortable with.

A few papers later, Mark was surprised at one of the answers that a student had given. He had a question in his exam that had asked for the benefits of electronic commerce to customers. He had taught in class that the benefits were lower prices, more selections, more convenience in shopping, and so forth.

The student had written, 'It allows for more discretionary purchases such as ...' She then went on to list out all of the products that she was purchasing through electronic commerce.

The answer was correct but Mark felt embarrassed when he read the answer. It was too much knowledge for him to know about a student's activities. She could have just put a period after purchases, and he would have considered her answer as complete. The rest of her paper was well done and so he ended up giving her a high grade for her exam.

He had to laugh at an answer that another student had given. Mark had wanted students to draw a HIPO diagram that would show all of the inputs, processes, and outputs for a business situation that he had described. It was obvious that the student did not know how to do this. He had instead drawn a picture of a hippo with an arrow going into his mouth for inputs, an arrow coming out of his butt for outputs, and an arrow pointing at his stomach for processing. Mark debated whether he should give the student at least a point for being so creative with his answer.

He also caught a few students who were using the questions as the answers. One of his exam rules was that the students could not do this. The first question on his exam had asked students to define what a Chief Information Officer was.

Some students had written, 'That is the officer who is in charge of information.'

That answer did not convince Mark that the students knew what the officer did. The correct answer would have been that the officer planned out the computer systems that a business should use in order to make them more efficient, as well as more competitive, in the marketplace.

He also noticed students who would then use that definition question in the last question when he asked them to give recommendations on how to improve a given business situation. The students were saying that you had to hire a Chief Information Officer, and were also putting in some of the other definition questions from the exam. There was a lot of information that was taught in his course this term, and the students could easily have suggested other methods if they understood the material.

However, only minor points were lost by students who did this but it was enough to move them into the next lower grade level. They would have received full marks if they had just spent a little more time on their exams, and thought through the course material more carefully.

Mark was about half way through his marking when his phone rang.

"Hi Mark. It's Cindy. How is your marking going for the midterm exams?"

"I have most of them marked already. How's your marking going?"

"I just finished. Do you want to take a break now and go out for some lunch?"

"That sounds fine. Should I meet you over at the new shopping mall again?"

"OK. Let's meet there in about 30 minutes near the main entrance."

Mark took his time in driving over there since he knew that Cindy was farther from the mall than he was. When he got there the parking lot was full so he had to park in the street beside the mall.

Cindy arrived a few minutes later and she appeared to be out of breath.

"Sorry I'm late. I couldn't find any parking, and so I had to park my car about a block away."

"I had the same problem. Would it be alright if we sat in the outdoors patio at the restaurant over there? It's such a warm day out with only a gentle breeze blowing."

Cindy readily agreed and he led her over to the patio and then seated her at a corner table. After they had placed their orders, he asked her, "How did you manage to mark your exams so fast? Your class is just as large as mine is."

"It was easy to mark the answers. I simply gave full points for all of the correct ones."

"What about partial points for answers? And don't you put in comments to explain why you took away marks?"

"I don't do that. My review next week will go through all of the questions and their answers."

"That's quite different from my way of thinking. I try to help the students along in any way that I can. I often think back to my own studies and on how I was graded. I also think about the struggles that I had sometimes when I was working because certain concepts were not reinforced in my studies."

While they sat enjoying their meals, Mark spent the next hour explaining about how his studies and his work experiences had helped to shape his own thoughts on education.

Cindy had never worked but she talked about her own study experiences as well. She had studied straight through university for a DBA since she had rich parents who had paid for all of her studies.

Her father had encouraged her to pursue business studies. He had even told her what courses to take. She had started with a Bachelor of Commerce degree, then an MBA degree, and finally a DBA degree. Her father had wanted her to focus on the applied study of existing business processes in a DBA, rather than on the research of new business processes in a PhD. There were two types of DBA programs. Her DBA was dissertation based. It had required that she solve an existing problem using sophisticated methods. Then she had had to defend her recommendations before a university committee.

There were also other DBA programs that were only course based. They were focused exclusively on lots of courses that dealt with advanced business processes. The students in course based DBA programs did not have to produce a final dissertation paper that solved an actual business problem. Course based DBA programs were preferred by senior managers. They just wanted to acquire the knowledge of advanced methods that they could use in their businesses.

Because Cindy did all of her studies at the same university, it was easy for her to get accepted into their masters and doctoral programs. Her parents lived near the university, and so they had encouraged her to go to it instead of to another university in a remote city. The university had then offered her a teaching position as soon as she had finished off all of her schooling.

Mark was reluctant to get back to grading papers after their meal ended. However, he knew that if he didn't finish them today then it would probably be early next week before he had the energy again to finish them. He bid a pleasant goodbye to Cindy, who said that she wanted to wander around the mall for the rest of the afternoon.

When he drove up to his home, he could see that several neighbors were out working on their yards. One of them had his dog outside with him. Mark wandered over to play with the dog for a while and to chat with his neighbor.

"Hi Mark. Where've you been these past few days?"

"I've been occupied over at the university giving exams and now I'm stuck in my home grading all of the papers. What've you been up to?"

"My company just expanded their operations due to all of the new contracts that they got. Do any of your students want some part time jobs? We would even be willing to hire a few of them if they are graduating this term."

"That's wonderful news. I'll pass it along to them. You may get some calls over the next week or two."

Mark thanked his neighbor for the information, played with the dog for a few more minutes, and then entered his own home. He made a mental note to himself that he would have to do some work on his own yard after he was finished with his marking.

The next few papers that he graded were very well done. There were a few mistakes that were made but one paper managed to get 100 %. Mark considered putting a gold star on the paper, like he used to get in primary school for some of his tests. He didn't know of any professors that did that, and so he just wrote 'well done' on the paper, and then pulled out the next paper.

This paper turned out to be difficult to grade. The student had started with a question in the middle of the exam, followed by one from the beginning, and then another from near the end of the exam. The rest of the questions were sprinkled in random order throughout the paper. Mark had to make up a chart to keep track of the questions that had been answered, and he then discovered a couple of questions that had been missed completely. It took him nearly three times as long to grade that paper compared to the other papers that he had already graded.

He would have to remind his students in the future to put their answers in the same order as his questions. Otherwise, he would consider deducting points for the extra time that he had to spend on marking such a paper.

He was starting to see a lot of papers now that got in the 90's and another one that got 100 %. For sure, there were a few papers in the beginning that got in the 90's but those were from the brightest students in his class, and so they did not need to spend the full time on the exam.

The last three papers that had to be graded were from the student who had arrived late for the exam, from the student who had brought in the friendly dog, and from Marcia.

He graded the other papers first because he was interested in reading the comments that Marcia had said that she had put into her exam. The marks were decent for the other papers, although he was surprised by the student who had come in late. That student had managed to get a grade in the 80's, but Mark felt that the student could have done much better if he had instead spent the full amount of time on the alternative exam the next day.

At this point, Mark was now ready to open up Marcia's paper.

Her answers were well thought out and there was only one mistake that he could find. Her comments were on the last page as he turned it over. They started with *Dear Professor* and then got more intimate the more that he read. He would have to talk to her about it and he wondered if students from his own time were like Marcia. He had been so busy studying when he went to university that he had rarely interacted with those around him.

Overall, he found that the exam papers were well done and that they were a considerable improvement over the previous quizzes and assignments that he had received so far. Next week, he would review the exam and then get the students started on their group project for his course.

He figured that he had a couple of hours of daylight left so he set down all of the papers and headed outside.

He first checked around the windows of his house. He found a few spots where the birds had tried to get in, and so he resealed them. He had read that if you hang some shiny disks on trees near your house then the birds will stay away. He had also heard about something called a bird spider device with flexible metallic spokes that was meant to be installed on a roof. Supposedly, it scared birds away as it rotated and moved with the wind. He would have to try those.

When he checked out the roof of his house he also discovered some damage on his chimney. He suspected that it was probably just the squirrels that were playing around up there. Then, while he was raking the leaves in his backyard, he saw a raccoon suddenly poke its head out from under his deck to watch him.

This brought back instant memories for him.

When he was a small child, a raccoon had wandered into his room. That raccoon was very friendly and very curious.

He had kept it well fed, and had played with it daily. He had fed it hamburgers and hot dogs. He had figured that if they were good enough for him then they were good enough for the raccoon. He had also given it some fruits and vegetables, and occasionally he had even managed to catch some grasshoppers for it to eat.

Then one day the raccoon had just wandered away, and he had never seen it again. It was a few months after that that he had been given a dog by his father.

However, as he approached this raccoon, it hissed and snarled at him. So it wasn't as friendly as his pet raccoon! He left it alone for now but entered his home to call the city. They said that they could send out a wildlife officer in the next day or so to trap it. The city official assured him that it was a humane trap, and that once the raccoon was caught, then it would be released back into the countryside.

That evening, Mark thought back on his life so far, the journeys that he had been through, the rewards that he had received, and the setbacks that he had encountered. He wondered what other choices he could have made if he had known then what he knew now.

Chapter 12: Past Rewards

Nothing is impossible to a willing mind. (Lao Tzu)

Mark encountered his first major challenge in life when, due to poor scheduling by his undergraduate university, he was forced to write all five of his final exams back to back over the space of only two days. It had already been a hard year for him.

He had jumped immediately to second year at the university after challenging all of the exams for the first year courses. As a result, he did not have a chance to form friendships with the other new students. Everyone in second year had already established their social groups in the prior year.

The university had scheduled exams for Mark in the morning, early afternoon, late afternoon, and then again the following morning and afternoon. By the time that Mark entered his third exam that first day, he realized that he had confused it with another exam that he would be writing the next day. One of the exams was for microeconomics, and the other exam was for macroeconomics. He had reviewed the wrong set of notes the previous night!

Although he was familiar with the material, he knew that he would have been better prepared if he had studied the right set of notes.

He was already on edge from all of the bitter black coffee that he had drank the previous night, in order to try to stay awake while he studied for his exams. He had had only a few hours of restless sleep before his first set of exams. Now he had to do all of this all over again to prepare for the next day.

By the end of the second day of his exams, he was bushed. He went back to his housing at the university and crashed for twelve hours solid.

A few days later, while he was packing up his belongings to head back home to help out his father over the summer, he received a call from someone at the university's administration office.

"Mark Klepin? We heard some good reports from your professors on your academic enthusiasm. We have a project that we'd like you to work on over the summer for us. It would pay twice what you are making now for marking papers, and we could let you stay in the university residence for free.

"We need a database system built that will allow us to match up students with relevant jobs when they graduate.

"Would you be interested?"

Mark had to pause for a moment.

His father was expecting him home over the summer to help with the family business, but he knew that his father would not be paying him. He hated to disappoint him but he really needed the money. He wanted to be able to finish his university studies. He did not want to have to quit near the end of it because he had run out of money.

"Are you still there, Mark?"

"Yes. I'll take your job. When can I start?"

"Can you come over to the administration offices this Friday to sign all of the paperwork, and then start looking at what we'll need?"

"I'll be there. Thank you for this opportunity."

Now came the hard part. Mark needed to call his father to explain what he had done.

"Hello? Father, how is Mom doing? I think that I'll be staying at the university this summer. They have offered me a great job to help them out for a few months. This means that I won't be able to come back home. I knew that you were counting on my help."

"Mark! Why do you want to do that? You know that you'll just be coming back here after your graduation. You might as well start learning the family business in more detail sooner, rather than later. It'll do you some good."

"I might want to stay in the city after my graduation. They have lots of interesting technical jobs here. I'll still see you this weekend before I start working here full time. And I'll still have next summer to get together with you."

His father was gravely disappointed. He had been hoping that Mark would grow tired of university once he got there. His father had built up a successful business without a university education and he was sure that any determined person could do the same. He had thought that Mark had shared his enthusiasm for running a business.

"All that I can say Mark is that you'll have to choose what you think is best for yourself in life. I still think that you could do very well working with me in the family business."

"I know Father. But give me a chance to find my own way in life. I need to follow my dreams for a while to see where they will take me."

Mark started to wonder if he had made the right choice after he had finished his call to his father. He had been exposed to a lot of ideas in his studies, and in all of the readings that he had done. However, he really did want to explore the world to see all that it could offer him.

During that summer, he struggled to learn several new techniques as he built the job matching database for the university.

At one point, the university's technical staff called him in and gave him a *big byte* award for using up all of the space on the university's computers. He had accidently entered the wrong commands into their main computers, with the result that it had allocated all of its space to his project. The university had to shut down for a day until they figured out what had happened.

That project was a success, and he was now able to enter his next year of studies with some practical experience that would help him to understand the concepts that were presented in his courses.

He never did get back the next summer to help out in the family business. Another opportunity came up for part time work at a new computer manufacturing company. That job enabled him to pay for the remainder of his studies.

Before he started his part time job with them later the next summer, he saw an advertisement from a large university in his country that was recruiting students from across his country. They had arranged with universities throughout China to send students to China, so that they could show the students around for a few weeks. China wanted the world to have a better impression of their educational systems and of their economy. They wanted it from students' viewpoints. The only requirement was that the students that came had to obtain their own funding for the trip.

Mark immediately applied, even though he didn't have any money for such a trip. He then spent the next two weeks canvasing businesses in the area to see if they could help sponsor him for such a trip. Many were quite interested.

"How would you like me to help you out if you sponsor me?" Mark asked them.

"Do you think that you could make up a report for us, which details China's business practices, manufacturing processes, and educational reforms? Such knowledge will help us to be more competitive."

"I would be happy to do that. I will also try to bring back some business contacts for you."

With only a few days before the trip was to begin, he finally scraped together enough money to get approved for the trip. It was the trip of a lifetime! It was the first time that he had gotten out of his own country, and it motivated him to get a job later that would allow him to do more travel around the world.

When he got back, he ended up getting on the dean's list of exceptional students at the university during his final year of studies. He was not able to become the best student, like he wanted, but he certainly tried. He still learned enough from his university studies, and from his own studies, to get a great job when he graduated.

After a year of working, Mark's income doubled due to his success in analyzing business systems for clients that needed their operations improved. He also challenged as many industry certification exams as he could during that time, and he passed all that he attempted.

Certification exams are used by businesses to verify that people have the required skills that are needed. There are exams for business topics as well as for technical topics. The exams are made up by groups, who are themselves made up of major businesses, manufacturers, and computer associations. Many of these groups have been around for decades, and their members come from thousands of businesses around the world.

The exams themselves are conducted in sealed rooms with no computers in them. No notes or books are allowed in the rooms. Businesses want to verify that people know the basic skills that are required of them. They do not want people who only know how to search for the answers to basic problems that they have to solve.

Businesses want professional people who have appropriate skills that can be confirmed.

Anyone who leaves during a certification exam is not allowed to return to the exam room. The exams were usually three hours long, but Mark once wrote one that was five hours long. Needless to say, examinees need to go to the washroom before an exam, and to cross their legs during an exam.

Mark jokingly asked the examiners one time, "Can I bring a cup into the exam room...for you know what?"

"Certainly not!" they promptly replied.

The exams are made up of about 200 questions, and so examinees only have about a minute to analyze each question, and to then pick one of five possible answers. You need at least 75 % to pass the exams, and the examiners do not tell you which questions you got wrong if you failed the exam. For that matter, they don't even say which ones you got right if you passed the exam. They don't want people telling their friends how to pass the exams. There are also cameras in the exam room, recording everyone who is taking the tests to make sure that no one is referring to notes, or helping others.

It usually takes most people a few weeks, or even a few months, to prepare for the certification exams. And this assumes that they have years of training in the skills that they are getting certified in. However, anyone who has studied the appropriate material can take the exams. Preparing for certification exams allows anyone to focus their studies so that they learn a lot more than those who just randomly discover new business ideas and technologies.

And Mark loved to study to learn new ideas that he could use!

The certification exams are usually voluntary, but they are strongly recommended by most professionals. Most businesses gave promotions, along with pay increases, to those that obtain certifications. Some businesses won't even hire people unless they have certain certifications.

In the year in which he obtained his own certifications, Mark was promoted to a senior analyst role in spite of his young age.

He was then sent over to a major client to help their operations people trace some problems in their computer systems. They supported a few hundred people at the corporate office. Their computer room was state of the art, with the latest equipment, a modern fire suppression system, and a monitoring system to detect anything that happened within it.

After a manager gave Mark a tour of the facilities, he told him to wait in the computer room. He wanted to get some paperwork for him to look over.

Mark was sitting at a desk that had an older computer on top of it. While he was examining it, he heard a large bang from behind him. Turning around, he could see that a power transformer had overloaded and that there was now a blazing fire, along with considerable smoke, coming from it. An acrid smell began filling the room. Immediately, a gas started hissing out from the fire suppression system in the ceiling to smother the fire.

But it would smother him as well!

He tried the door but it had auto-locked when the fire had started. In desperation he used his past martial arts training, from clubs at the university that he had attended, to try to kick the door open but it would not budge. With only seconds before he was overcome by the gas, he went with *Plan B*.

He grabbed the older computer on the desk, tossed it through the window of the computer room, and then dove through after it. He used a Judo break fall, which he had also learned, to safely roll back up to a standing position amid all of the broken glass.

Alarms were blaring and everyone was staring at him.

One of the workers said to him, "I've often hit that old computer in frustration, but I like your idea better. Just toss it through the window. I guess that we'll have to buy a replacement for it after all."

"Glad that I could be of assistance," Mark said.

Once the fire was out and all of the excitement had died down, some of the workers then tried to get back into the computer room. The door was jammed! It seemed that Mark's kicks had bent its frame enough that it could not be opened now.

The manager said to him, "Are your software skills as strong as your hardware skills?"

Mark could only smile and then look around in embarrassment.

Later that year, he had the opposite problem at a different client site. He was in a meeting going over the designs of their new system when everyone heard shouting coming from the computer area. Upon rushing over there, they could see that a water pipe above the computer room had broken. It was spraying water everywhere, and the floor was totally soaked by this time.

"Mark, get in there and shut down our systems so that they don't get damaged."

"What about me getting damaged, from all of the power that is in there?" Mark exclaimed.

He had a better idea.

He contacted some experts that he knew in the city, and then he had the experts issue an emergency power down for the industrial complex that the client was in. The proper way would have been to track down a janitor, and then to send him down to the locked power room that was in the basement. From there, the power to the building could have been shut down. But it was faster to have the city issue a software command to the power substation for the building, in order to shut down the power.

Then Mark directed the client to shut down the power to their systems so that they wouldn't get damaged when the power came back on. When the city restored power to the area then he used the client's backup networks and systems to switch all of their operations over to them.

He asked the client, "Why in the world would you install a computer room under a water pipe?"

"It was OK when we set it up. One of the contractors must have installed that pipe at a later time when the executive showers were set up."

Mark was thinking of a few choice comments that he could make, but he held his tongue.

'*What next?*' he wondered.

There were many celebrations over the ensuing years, as system after system was successfully designed and built for clients.

Mark could recall one such celebration that occurred at an engineering company's head office site after a new system had been installed for them. Some of his co-workers had wandered into the computer room, and one of them had brought in a champagne bottle. There were already some glasses on top of the cabinet that held the main computers. Mark volunteered to pour the champagne but while he was pouring the champagne into the glasses, he dropped the bottle. The champagne rapidly drained down into the cabinet and then began soaking the computers inside of it.

Everyone became alarmed as sparks started to fly from the computers. Then the printers attached to the system stopped working, the screens attached to them became blank, and finally all of the main computers just shut down.

Their boss came bursting into the room. "What did you do?" he shouted at everyone.

He could see what Mark had done and then he pointed at a sign that read 'No food or drink in the computer room.' With annoyance, he said, "Can't you read?"

The party in the building was still in full swing and no one else had noticed yet what had happened. Mark's boss then sent him and several of his co-workers scurrying from the room, in order to buy hair dryers from the local stores in the city. It was a desperate move.

When everyone came back, they were all involved in blowing hot air onto the computer systems to try to dry them out. They kept at it for an hour. Then, with fingers crossed, they turned on the main computers and watched in wonder as the systems restarted, and carried on where they had left off. The new systems were truly amazing!

Another embarrassing moment occurred for Mark a couple of years later.

He had recently been involved in a new credit authorization system for a national retailer. He was asked if he could modify that system so that their customers could submit payments at the store, for items that they had previously billed to their account.

Billings were used by corporate customers that wanted to pay for everything later from a monthly statement. Residential customers just paid as they purchased items.

Mark knew that this change could save a lot of paperwork at the head office of the retailer. They were currently being flooded with payments each month that were being sent in by their corporate clients. It would be so much easier if these payments could just be processed locally by the closest stores.

It was a very easy change for Mark to make to the system. The normal procedure would have been for him to verify his change with a single store first, then a few more, and finally to give the change to all of the stores. But he felt confident that he knew what he was doing, and so he sent the change to all of the stores that night.

Within an hour of the stores opening the next day, the entire credit authorization system shut down. Mark had overlooked a small detail in how the system worked. It took a few hours to resolve the problem and to get everything working again. In the meantime, the stores had to go back to processing all types of customer payments on some hand written forms that they had kept around from many years ago.

Mark learned his lesson the hard way that day. Always follow procedures!

An even more memorable moment occurred for him a month later.

He was asked to phone every one of the store managers to obtain certain figures from their computer systems. There were hundreds of calls to make. It would take him an entire month to get all of the figures. He was sure that he was being punished.

He had seen a lot about how the client's systems worked. And he knew a lot about computer systems. There was a program on the client system that was used to install new programs from their head office.

Mark first wrote a program to obtain the necessary figures from a store, and then he made it send the results back to him. He then tricked the program at the client's head office into sending his program to all of the stores, in order to add it as part of their daily processing.

Within a day, he had all of the required figures that he had been asked to obtain. He walked back into his boss's office to present them to him.

"Here are the results that you wanted Bob."

"There is no way that you could have obtained these in a day. Who helped you?"

"I did it myself. I encouraged the client's systems to do the work for me."

He then launched into a detailed discussion of how the client systems worked and how he had used them to obtain the necessary information. His boss thought that Mark's approach was brilliant, and praised him for his ingenuity.

After that, Mark was assigned to numerous other projects that needed innovative solutions. He encountered many challenges over the years, but also many rewards for the work that he was doing.

One time, the building of a small construction company caught fire and burned to the ground. All of their computer systems were gone. Mark was sent over there to coordinate all of the activities that would be needed to get their systems going again.

He was able to persuade the manufacturer of their computer to deliver a new system to them that day at a new location. He then spent all night and most of the next day restoring their computer programs, as well as the data from the backups that they had made.

During his time at the construction company, he discussed his own construction experiences with the owner. When he was a kid, his father had spent several years building a new estate home for his family. He could remember that all of them, including the uncles, had helped out whenever they could. During that time, he was busy trying to help out wherever it was needed.

Getting the computer systems at the construction company up and going was the first time that he had worked forty hours straight since waking up. There would be a few more times like this over the course of his career.

A few months later, he received an emergency call from a franchised retail store late at night. He was just getting ready to go to sleep when the call arrived.

"Hi Mark. We could really use your help. We just installed new point of sale cash register machines but our computer won't read the daily sales from them. We need this fixed before we open up for business in the morning."

"OK. Give me 30 minutes to get ready. I will see you shortly."

Mark quickly changed into a suit and headed over to the store. He ended up being there all night working on the problem.

He eventually had to call the manufacturer of the cash registers, in order to persuade them to make an update for the computer chips that they used. He needed the communication speed of their chips adjusted, along with the control language that they used. Luckily, they were able to send him the updated software for their computer chips, a scant couple of hours before the client's store had to be opened.

Mark wished that the client had initially called him up when they were setting up the new technologies that they had wanted to use. He had developed a reputation among businesses over the years as a trouble shooter.

As it turned out, it was only a twenty four hour workday this time since he had woken up the previous day. But it was still a long day, and he could do without all of the *work around the clock* events.

Another time, he received a call on the weekend from a larger franchised retail store. It was the end of the year, and they were closed to count their entire inventory. Most retailers did this to see if any inventory had become lost, damaged, or stolen, since the last time that they had counted it. This particular retailer had over a hundred thousand items to count.

The counts were compared to the computer records to locate any discrepancies. The problem was that their computer system would not interface to the counting devices that they were using. They could not figure out how to get the data into their computer. They needed this resolved before Monday morning.

It took Mark a day and a half to resolve all of their problems to get their data into their computer systems. First, he had to make up a custom cable so that their counting devices could be plugged into their main computer. Then he had to make up special software to read the data from their devices and to put it into their databases.

The data also turned out to be in an unknown format. By the time that he finished working with everyone to get their counts updated correctly in their databases, it was another forty hour workday!

Mark wondered if university professors had the same kinds of challenges and rewards that he was facing.

Chapter 13: The Feedback

If one person gets there with one try, try ten times. If another succeeds with a hundred tries, make a thousand. (Lao Tzu)

It had been an interesting weekend for Mark. He had completed grading all of the midterm exams and it was now time to give them back to the students to go over the results. Some of the students would be very pleased with their results, but he could think of a couple of them that would be unhappy with their marks.

"Good morning, everyone!"

"Good morning, sir. Did you finish marking our exam papers?"

"I did. Should I give them back or should I just tear them up?"

"Were they that bad?" asked one student.

"Actually, most of them were pretty good. Everyone passed except for one person."

"Are you looking at me, Professor?" a worried student said.

"Don't worry. You passed but you and everyone else could have done a little better. A lot of you rushed through the exam and you made mistakes that you shouldn't have."

"What was the average mark, Professor?"

"Overall, the class average was 89 %. I am quite pleased with that. It is much better than the last quiz, which averaged 77 %. This is a difficult course but I have seen a lot of improvement over the weeks in the assignments that you have been turning in."

"Did anyone get 100 % on it?"

"Two people did get 100 % but there were several people who also got in the 90's on it."

"That sounds hopeful. Can we see our papers now?"

"I will start handing them out in a moment. There are comments in the exam papers but I will spend time going through all of the questions, and then some possible answers that could have been given for them."

Mark spent the next few minutes calling out student names and handing back their papers. Most seemed pleased with their marks but he did notice scowls on a few of the faces.

One student put up his hand and asked, "Can I have you look at this question and the marks that you gave me?"

"Hold that thought. Let me go through all of the questions and their answers first. Then, if anyone still needs their marks clarified, they can see me during the break. However, note that I did see some rather unusual answers in this exam.

"For example, one student told me exactly what she was buying online with her home computer, as an electronic commerce benefit for discretionary purchases. I didn't need to see that level of detail in the exam."

There were some smiles and high fives in the room, as Mark's students looked around at each other to try to determine who had given such an answer.

"Contrary to this, other students said things like third generation software programs are more advanced than first generation software programs. Such answers are much too vague. You need to give some definitions, or to explain your answer in more detail, in order to get credit for knowing the answer."

Over the next hour, Mark carefully went through every question, and explained the answers that could have been given. He also tried to show every step that was involved in the calculation questions.

"Let's take a short break now before we form the groups for the project assignment. Then we will look at the material in the next chapter."

Only one student approached Mark at that time to discuss the last question on the exam and the way that he had solved it. Mark could now see the student's point of view. He awarded a few more points on that exam paper and updated his grade sheets to reflect the changes. No one else approached him during the break, and so he decided that he could continue with the class.

"Does anyone have any questions on the material to this point?"

"Now that we have seen the answers, it all seems so easy now," said Tim.

"I think that you will find that the group project, that all of you will have to work on next, will further clarify the material in this course. I need five members per group. I will give you a few minutes to determine who you would like to be in a group with. Anyone without a group can see me at the front of the room."

Mark noticed that most of the students were getting together with those that they knew. A few students seemed to be abandoned by the groups that were forming, and so he waved them over to him.

"I will assign the groups for you to work in. There are enough of you to create two groups. I would like to form groups where the students have different majors, so that your solutions are more complete. Give me a moment to determine which of you to put into each group."

While the students chatted amongst themselves, Mark consulted his registration lists to create the two new groups. He also tried to get a mix of genders in the groups to balance out the various viewpoints. Finally, he was satisfied with the group members and sent them back to their seats. He also asked the other groups to give him a list of their members.

"Please remember that you will be working on a group project. Everyone is expected to contribute equally to the project. If any group finds that they are having issues with their members then they can contact me, and I will remove those members from their group. It is a lot harder to do a group project on your own rather than doing just 20 % of it. Please help out your team mates."

There was silence in the room.

Several students glanced around at their classmates. Some students were pointing at others and shaking their fingers at them. Mark could see them silently saying to the others, *he means you.*

"This project will be a significant portion of your course grade. It will allow you to apply most of the material in the course to solve an actual business problem. You need to identify a business that is having issues with their efficiency or with their competitiveness in the market. Then you will plan out a solution for them and recommend some technologies that they could use to help themselves."

"How long do we get to do all of that?"

"There are still two months left in this term. You will need to submit a paper on your group work before the final exam is given. Your papers should describe the details of the company that you are investigating, solutions that you have identified, and the time and cost for implementing your solutions. I strongly suggest that you start on your projects immediately."

There were some murmurs in the room.

Mark felt that the students had gotten the idea now. He had seen in previous terms where some groups had waited until the last week, or two, in order to attempt to do the work on their projects. It tended to overwhelm them when they did that. The poorer quality on that rushed work resulted in them getting lower grades.

"You can see me in my office if you want my ideas on companies that you can investigate, and some technologies that you can use to create solutions for them. I have consulted with many of them before. I am quite familiar with their operations."

"That'd be wonderful, sir," said Marcia. "I'll come up and see you right after the class."

"Make sure that you bring your group members with you. Remember that this is a group project and that everyone is expected to contribute to it equally."

Marcia looked disappointed but Mark figured that she just wanted to ask him other questions, and not group related questions. He would have to deal with her issues soon, rather than later.

He remembered that there was a technology competition in the city the next month. He felt that it would be a great opportunity for his students to show off their skills.

"I want to remind everyone that there is a contest next month at the conference center downtown. Any college or university student can drop in to solve the technology problems that they will be giving out. There will be prizes for those that solve the most problems in the least amount of time. I encourage all of you to try it out."

There seemed to be a lot of eager faces in the room.

"After that contest, there will be a technology conference in the following week. You will need to register for that and I would suggest that all of you do that. There are special discounts for students. You will learn about the new technologies that are available for businesses to use, and this will definitely benefit you in your future careers."

Now every face in the room was full of eagerness and anticipation.

"OK. Now let's proceed with the material in the next chapter."

Mark started by showing the students how the material in previous chapters had identified solutions for specific parts of a business. There were solutions to do with receiving goods, shipping goods, selling goods, processing orders, and accounting for business activities.

He then elaborated on how all of the various solutions could be integrated using enterprise systems. He explained how a single entry into a computer system would send its data into all of the related systems. His students could see how all of this integration worked from the diagram that he was drawing on the board for financial systems.

Orders would send their data into the sales system, in order that management could analyze them; into the inventory system, in order to lower the on hand quantities; into the general ledger system, in order to record the business activity; into the accounts receivable system, in order to record customer charges; and into the accounts payable system, in order to record taxes which were due to the government.

Once he had all of the processes summarized on the board, he turned to his computer system to illustrate how to integrate several software tools to make all of this happen.

While he was doing this, he noticed some unusual activity on one of his monitors.

The university had installed special software last term that allowed the instructors to monitor all of the computer activity in their classrooms. The intent of this was so that student work on problems and examples could be seen from the front of the room.

Some students were reluctant to raise their hands to ask for help when they ran into difficulties. The new monitors gave instructors the option to wander towards the computer that was identified, and then to just casually notice that a student was having issues so that they could help them out.

Mark could see that one of the students was doing some shopping on his computer.

The new monitoring software also allowed instructors to display what they were seeing onto the main projector for the class, along with the student name that the display came from. It was intended when students wanted to display one of their solutions for the class, but Mark had other ideas on his mind today.

"So tell me Tim. What do cars have to do with enterprise systems?"

Everyone could see Tim's name displayed on the main projector, along with the cars that he was viewing. Then they turned their heads to look at Tim.

It was an embarrassing moment for Tim who tried to stutter his way through an explanation.

In later classes, Mark noticed that all of his students always stayed focused on his lectures. Word also spread quickly around the university after that, and other professors told him that students paid more attention in their classes too.

One of the students in his current class put up her hand.

"Yes, Emilia?"

"These enterprise systems seem to be quite complex. Do we need to remember the features in the different software tools for the final exam?"

"I am glad that you brought that up. You only need to be aware of the concepts associated with them. Focus on the advantages and disadvantages of them along with the business areas that they can be used for. You may want to recommend these systems to companies that you work for later."

"Thanks, Professor."

The remainder of the lecture that day went better than he had expected.

After he wrapped up the class, Mark noticed that the groups were already getting together to discuss the projects that they wanted to do. That reminded him of how little socializing he had done in his own life. He wondered what kind of solutions his students would recommend for businesses. He looked forward to seeing them.

Chapter 14: Socializing

You will never do anything in this world without courage.
(Aristotle)

Mark led a relatively quiet life in the small town where he grew up. There was nothing for him to do in the evenings except to study or to visit relatives. On weekends, he would help out on one of his uncles' farms or in his father's business. On rare occasions, his parents would visit the nearby city. Mark knew from those trips, and from his own readings in the local library, that there was a lot more to life if he wanted it.

And he did want it!

He never did get a chance to participate in team sports. He never even learned to swim, not even to this day. But he did enjoy getting out on a boat whenever friends or family went to a nearby lake. He never got seasick. Much later in his life he often went out on sailboats on rough water around islands in the middle of the world's oceans. He thoroughly enjoyed the tossing of the boats in the waves.

There was one year that his father saw an advertisement for a new type of watercraft, called a Jet Ski. It was too expensive for him, and so his father decided that he could just make his own one. He got hold of an old snowmobile, some pontoons, and a boat propeller. He took the track and skis off of the snowmobile, mounted the pontoons on each side of it so that it would float, and hooked the propeller and steering up to a gearbox that he had installed underneath the snowmobile. It looked really cool!

They took the *water mobile* to a nearby lake to test it out.

"What is that?" someone asked.

The officials in the area were not even sure if they needed a boating license, or a snowmobile license, for it.

Amazingly, the contraption floated, and it was able to putter around the lake. It was not fast enough to pull a water skier but Mark still had a great time using it. It drew quite a crowd, and he became the envy of everyone around him.

That first day, he spent hours on the lake, playing with his *water mobile*. He ended up paying for his pleasure with a severe sun burn that he received over most of his body. But he felt that it had been worth it!

His parents lived on an estate that was a mile outside of the small town, and he often ran to school rather than wait for the school bus. He did the same thing at the end of the day to return home, and sometimes during the lunch hour as well to visit with his mom.

There was one morning when he encountered a cute little fox with a big bushy tail on the trail that he used. He froze and just stared at the fox for a minute while it also froze and stared back at him. He was considering whether he should dig his school books out from his backpack, and then proceed to throw them at the fox to scare it away. Luckily, the fox soon lost interest in him and then it just ran off into the bushes.

His running had prepared him for competing in several school track events, but this was about as close as he ever got to sporting events while he was in high school. He did win a few events, and so he knew what that feeling was like.

So he could not wait to get out of the small town to attend university at the nearby city. He was sure that there would be lots of activities to try out, or even to see, in between his study times.

The first sport that caught his eye at the university was fencing. He could remember seeing sword fighting movies when he was a kid, and he was always fascinated by the movements that were made in those movies. The university had a fencing club where they taught the use of the foil, the epee, and the sabre.

Foils were stabbing weapons and the targets were the chest, abdomen, and back. Epees were also stabbing weapons but the entire body was a target. Experts said that they were like real weapons because they were much heavier, and because you could attack any part of your opponent.

But Mark was drawn to the sabre, which was a slashing weapon like those that he had seen in the movies. The sabre could be used in fencing to attack any part of the body above the waist, including the arms and the head.

The instructor who ran the fencing school looked like he was ready to retire (or even to die) but he moved like greased lightning. No one could see him move when he attacked. He used to be on the Olympic team in his country when he was much younger.

Even though Mark wanted to start with the sabre, the instructor forced him to learn the foil first in order that he could perfect his footwork, his hand movements, and his sensitivity to fencing movements. Mark found that he had a natural talent for it and so he was soon introduced to the epee. It felt just like a big foil to him, but the first time that he got stabbed with it, he knew that it was radically different.

"Ow! That hurt!"

"Pay attention, Mark. The epee does not bend like the foil when you strike with it."

Then a few minutes later, he was hit in a different way. "Ow! Now you're poking my feet!"

"Anything is a target. Watch where you're stepping. Watch what I'm doing."

Next he got struck on the wrist, which caused him to drop his epee.

"If you think this hurts, just wait until I start training you on the sabre."

Mark had to endure some brutal training for the next few months with both the foil and the epee before the instructor felt that he was ready for the sabre. The sabre was normally used for slashing but it could also be used for stabbing, as Mark was to learn later.

The first time that he picked up a sabre, Mark attempted to make large arm movements like he had seen in pirate movies. None of his strikes could hit his opponents and they always slashed his arms.

"Watch me Mark," his instructor said. Mark noticed that his sabre was positioned in front of his body and slightly to one side. Whenever he blocked a strike, he rotated the blade and made minor movements. Then he seemed to just reach forward to either slash or stab his opponents.

"Put your mind at the tip of your sword and not on your body. Stand like I do Mark. Follow me as I rotate my sabre to the different blocking positions in preparation for attacking my opponent. Then follow my striking movements."

Mark spent a few months perfecting the blocks and strikes of the sabre. He often went back to his room at the university after fencing classes with red slashes on his arms and body. Other students were starting to wonder why he had bruises on his arms, and so he had to resort to wearing long sleeved shirts whenever he went to his regular classes.

Starting the next year, he competed in a number of fencing competitions. His instructor made him enter the foil, epee, and sabre competitions, even though Mark preferred to only compete with the sabre. He had felt like a pirate at that time!

One day his instructor showed him a unique way to hold his sabre that was only used in honor duels from ancient times. It guaranteed that he would get in a first strike since honor duels stopped once that strike was made. He was warned to only use it for his last strike in competitions, because his opponents would quickly learn how to counter it once they had seen it. Mark found that it took nerves of steel to execute the movement, because all of his instincts told him to do something else.

He continued his fencing training, and fencing competitions, all through his time at the university. He also competed whenever he could for a few years after he graduated.

There was one incident that scared the living daylights out of him!

It was the final bout of a sabre fencing match and Mark made a daring lunge at the head of his opponent. The blade of his sabre managed to go under the protective mask of his opponent when he tried tilting his head back to avoid the strike. Mark felt resistance in his sabre, and then he saw it come out of the back of his opponent's mask.

His opponent froze! Mark froze! His opponent's eyes opened wide. Mark's eyes opened wide. Some blood started trickling down the blade of his sabre. Mark's eyes opened even wider!

There was a collective gasp from the audience.

Someone shouted, "Don't move!"

The judges and some concerned audience members rushed over. They slowly removed the mask from Mark's opponent. There was a long cut along the side of his neck but nothing that was life threatening. After that incident, Mark competed less and less but he still dropped into fencing schools once in a while.

During his years at the university, Mark also developed an interest in the martial arts. There were lots of clubs and he tried out as many styles as he could. He tried out Judo, Karate, and Aikido, as well as Boxing and Wrestling. He didn't do so well in them since he was not athletically inclined but he still persevered.

He found that he was always being thrown to the ground and had his limbs twisted in Judo and Wrestling. He was also thrown to the ground in Aikido, and the others in that class liked to twist joints as well. In Karate and Boxing, he developed bruises from all of the strikes and blocks.

Eventually he was drawn to the Chinese styles where he found that their flowing movements fit in with his physique and mentality. He also learned how to use some other types of swords, such as the straight sword, the broad sword, and the butterfly swords. He figured that he could now offer hair cutting services to other students if he could get them to stand still.

He managed to spend several hours a week on physical activities, between his fencing and his practice of Chinese martial arts. The rest of his time was spent in pursuing his academic studies, and in investigating various topics in the university's extensive library.

Unfortunately, or fortunately depending on how you looked at it, this left him with no time for socializing and for going out for parties, or for any of the other activities that the other students were enjoying. The limit of his socializing was the time that he spent in the clubs, and in the competitions for them.

He did have some regrets but his intensive academic and physical training at the university did help him later with his working life, and with his personal life, as it turned out. Mark ended up continuing with his martial arts training for many years after he had left the university.

He could recall a business trip that he made to China a few years after he had graduated. He was coming back late at night from a meeting, and the interpreter was with him. They had taken a shortcut back to the hotel, and they were stopped by a person with a knife.

Mark said, "Ask him what he wants." (As if he didn't know already!)

There was some angry chatter back and forth between the interpreter and the assailant.

Mark said, "I think I know what he wants but tell him that there are no police around here."

The interpreter looked confused but translated his statement. This time, there was some more angry shouting.

Mark finally said, "Now tell him that there is no one here to protect him!"

There was utter silence once this had been translated. The assailant looked him up and down and then glanced around. Then he just walked away.

Mark was not sure if he could have escaped unhurt that night, but he knew that his assailant would definitely have been hurt and in need of hospital care. He made a mental note to himself that night to stay away from shortcut routes in the future.

He did attend a lot of business and technology conferences every year. He had started this trend a few years after he had started working, and he had continued it into his later academic years. He even had the privilege of speaking at a few of those conferences.

He could recall one such conference where the audience was so enthralled by what he had presented, that they started shouting, "Three cheers for Mark! Hip, hip, hoorah!"

Several members from the audience had then came up on the stage after his talk, lifted him above their heads, and then carried him through the audience that was still chanting. It was one of the more exciting moments of his life. He wondered if everyone experienced the sense of belonging that he had felt that day at the conference.

Most of the socializing that he partook of during his working life was at company dinners that his consulting company hosted, or that their clients hosted. There was one year that he was invited by a successful client to join her staff at an exclusive chateau in the mountains.

Mark was just finishing his MBA and he had felt like celebrating.

The client had paid for all of the airfare and accommodations for her staff, as well as for Mark. It was a victory celebration for the client, and Mark only wished that he was invited to more of those gatherings. The business people always seemed to be celebrating something, or enthusiastically discussing future plans for the coming year.

It seemed to Mark that he was always working or studying new technologies. For sure, he went on lots of business trips to cities around the world, but his exploration time was limited in those cities due to pressing project deadlines.

He sometimes envied others when he heard them discussing the parties and sporting events that they had attended. The biggest parties that he had attended were his own wedding parties when he had married his first wife, and later when he had married his second wife. His first wife eventually divorced him to do her own consulting around the world, and he lost his second wife a few years after he had met her. He almost considered marrying again just so that he could have another big party.

The only other time that he could recall when several people were gathered around him was when he had gotten an appendix attack during a project that he had been rushing to complete. This had happened to him a short time before he had started his MBA studies. The client had told him that the project was urgent and that the deadline could not be missed. It was an extremely complicated project, and he had already faced many challenges while doing it.

After his collapse, the client said to him, "The project is not that urgent. You can complete it when you get well."

The client and most of his staff had visited him in the hospital. They were very concerned with his condition and everyone urged him to calm down. They all told him that the project could wait.

The story that they now told him, was a completely different tune from the one that Mark had been hearing throughout the project over the last few months.

He had honestly believed the client when he had told him that the project was critical, and that its deadline could not be moved. The client and his staff had pushed him every day of the project, and now they were telling him to just relax.

He couldn't believe the change in their attitude!

Mark vowed from that moment forward that he would now take the events in his life as they came. He would go back to seeking his own path through life, as he had done years ago when he had planned out how he could improve his life.

Chapter 15: The Assessment

Those who put forth their strength and keep back their weakness are like a deep river into which all the streams flow. (Lao Tzu)

It was the end of the term but there was still a ton of work to do. Mark needed to grade the final exams from all of his courses. He also had to grade the projects from his main course. He was looking at several days of grading work. Then he had to combine all of the grades from each student to come up with their overall grades. Each assignment and test was worth a different percent of the final grade, and so he would need to set up the calculations in a computer to let it determine the results.

It was so much easier when the university had provided marking assistants to all of the professors.

Everyone used to record their marks electronically on the campus computer systems. However, a few terms ago it had crashed and the marks for all of the students had been lost. The administrators at the university had had no choice but to give all of the students an A in all of their courses for that term. After that, Mark and every other instructor kept paper records of their grades. They also recorded them diligently in their home computers.

Mark and the other instructors were currently given three business days to submit all of their grades. They used to be given five business days which was just sufficient for grading all of their courses when the weekends were also used. That marking time had been shortened a few years ago. That meant that everyone had lost two business days for marking plus the extra weekend.

As Mark picked up the first of the final exams in his courses, and began to look at it, his phone rang.

"Hello?"

"Mark, this is Irene from the administration office. The dean has asked me to notify all instructors to tell them that he'd like the entire student grades submitted on Monday morning by 8 AM. I know that it is short notice, but the holiday season is coming up and we need to expedite this."

Mark wondered what was being expedited, the grades or the dean's vacation.

"Of course, Irene. I will do my best."

He could not believe it! In all of his years of teaching the grading deadlines had never been rushed. He liked to carefully consider all final tests and assignments so that he could add constructive comments into them, and so that he could look for any partial marks that he could give. Now he would only be able to look briefly at each paper that he marked.

He gave Cindy a call to get her reaction on it.

"Hi Cindy. I've just started marking my final papers. Is your university asking you to submit your grades earlier this term?"

"Not that I have heard of. I don't think that they can do that. The rules for everything are in the faculty handbook, and they're also in the university's charter."

"That's what I thought. But I just received a call from the dean's office. They want our grades submitted this Monday by 8 AM. That means that I'll only get the weekend to mark everything. I won't even get my three business days next week to spend on marking."

"That's not fair. Did they give you a reason? Do you want me to come over there and help you?"

"I would love your help but the privacy laws forbid other instructors from seeing student papers. Personally, I think that the dean is going on vacation early rather than the students going on vacation early and demanding that they get their grades immediately."

"Let me know how it goes Mark. I just started on my own marking as well. We can meet up later next week after all of the grading is behind us."

"Thanks Cindy. I'll stay in touch."

As he went back to his desk to continue marking, he seriously considered making up some rubber stamps for the most common situations that he saw. Things like *wrong symbol in diagram, wrong step in calculation, cannot use questions as answers,* and so forth. Then he could just rubber stamp the exam papers as he went through them. Come to think of it, that was a great idea! He would need to consider doing that for the next term.

The first few exam papers that he looked at were pretty decent. There were a few mistakes in them but he could see that the students had caught on to the material by the end of the term. Or they were just studying all night like he used to do!

Then he encountered some exams that had left answers blank. He could only shake his head when he saw this because he was only half way through the pile of exams. This meant that the students had just given up early rather than think through the problems for as long as they could. The university really did need a prep course for students to counsel them on exam methods, as well as on study tips.

He finally got through the complete set of exams by 9 PM that night. Mark decided that he would enter the grades into the computer in the morning when he was not so tired. For now, he just wanted to turn in early to get a good night's rest. He still had all of the project papers to mark during the next day.

The stack of project papers that greeting him in the morning was over a foot tall. He could have sworn that they had grown taller overnight! His students had obviously put in a lot of effort on them, and he did look forward to reading all of them.

'*Here goes another long day,*' he thought.

Some of the group projects were shorter than the others and so he decided that he would tackle them first. They would get him warmed up for the bigger project papers.

The first project that he looked at discussed the warehousing issues at a national retailer. The students were proposing an automated system that used robots to manage the warehouse, along with software that integrated all of the robotic sensors into the inventory systems at the head office. It was a brilliant solution even though the paper was shorter than the others that he still had to look at. He awarded full marks to that group paper.

A few papers later, another project that caught his eye concerned the scheduling of custom orders at a manufacturing company. Each of the company's customers had different requirements. The students had figured out how to efficiently distribute the orders throughout the factory floor to the different machinery on it. They lost some points, due to not including a timeline for implementing their solution, but overall the students had written a good project paper.

The final project paper that he looked at seemed to be impressive. It was the largest paper of all of the group papers, but when he opened it, Mark saw that most of it was composed of just sales reports from a retail operation. Looking further, he discovered that it was basically a marketing report for a software company that wanted retailers to buy its tools.

The students had obviously spent a lot of time researching it but they were still missing some key requirements from the project paper. They got a decent mark but they could have gotten a higher mark if they had spent equal amounts of time focusing on each part of their project.

Mark made sure to add in lots of comments on the project papers to justify the grades that he gave. The administrators at his university reserved the right to challenge the grades that were given. Instructors had to be able to prove why they gave high marks for papers that were turned in. This helped to maintain the quality of all final work that was submitted by the students.

The university would often gather some sample papers, remove the student names, and then use them in their meetings with businesses to show the depth of the work that their students were capable of. These often led to job offers for their students later on as well as recommendations for other topics that the businesses would like their students to learn about.

As a final step in his grading, Mark looked to see if any students were close to the next higher grade level.

He liked to further help out any students, who had given evidence that they were at least making an effort to cope with the material in a course. He looked for things like assignments that were turned in on time, for students who consistently arrived in class on time, for those that paid attention in class, and for those that used most of the exam time to carefully consider the answers that they had given. In those situations, he would round up the student's grade to the next level. Over the years, he had even managed to give passes to a number of struggling students by doing just that.

That night, he was finally able to enter the completed grades for all of his courses. Last week, he had managed to resolve all of Marcia's issues to her complete satisfaction, and he was able to give her a high grade in the course. Most of his students had done very well this term, and he was extremely pleased with their progress at the university.

He looked forward to the next term. In the following week, he would try to determine where he should take a vacation in the summer. He decided that Bill, who also taught in his department, might have some ideas.

"Hi Bill, this is Mark. Sorry to call you so late. But do you mind if I ask you where you went for your vacation last summer? I'm trying to get some suggestions for this year."

"I took the family on a great cruise last year. It was fantastic and very relaxing. Do you think that you'd be interested in trying out a cruise as well?"

"Actually, I'd thought about that a couple of years ago but I never got around to it. Do you have any recommendations?"

"There are so many choices now. Just call around and you'll be sure to find one that suits you."

"Thanks Bill. I think that I'll do just that and then I'll let you know how it was when I get back."

It ended up taking Mark a few days to go through all of the material from the various cruise lines. He had to consider the locations that they visited, the facilities that they offered onboard, the activities that they could arrange in their ports of call, and, of course, their pricing. He picked out a two week cruise that interested him. The cruise line had an opening for next month and so he took it.

He arranged to fly to the cruise ship's port a day early. He wanted to wander around the port before the cruise ship departed. When he got there he noticed that a company at the dock was offering rubber zodiac rafting tours of the surrounding bay areas. It looked like fun. He promptly signed up for one of their tours.

Everyone had to get into bright red sea survival suits. They were told that these would allow them to float if they got thrown out of the boat. The suits would also keep them warm until they could be rescued. Mark was beginning to think that the zodiac tour was not such a good idea after all!

He began to relax once they successfully got further out into the bay. Their tour started to pass some small islands with lots of trees and flowering bushes on them. He noticed an eagle in the water nearby that looked like it was swimming using a breast stroke.

"Why is that eagle swimming instead of flying?" he asked the guide.

"That is what happens when they dive down and catch a fish that is too big for them to lift out of the water. Then they have to flap their way over to the nearest shore. You could say that he bit off more than he could chew," the guide replied.

"I see. Then why is there a deer over there swimming between the shore and the island that we are approaching? Did he catch a fish too?"

"The deer in this area often swim out to the islands. We're not sure why they do that. There was one day when a boater brought one of them back to the port. He thought that he was rescuing the deer. We never did figure out how he got the deer out of the water and into his boat."

The rest of the tour was going well until they stopped near some logs that had a few black seals resting on them. The seals looked cute with their big eyes and long whiskers. While everyone was busy taking pictures of them, a young seal swam alongside their boat and slid over the side of it. He probably thought that their boat was a big log.

"Quick. Grab him. Corral him into a corner and then throw him back over the side," the guide shouted at them.

Mark could remember catching sheep on a farm. How hard could this be? When he grabbed the seal it was so slimy that he couldn't maintain his hold on it. It slipped from his grasp and slithered around the boat. It was barking at everyone while they all tried to catch it. Eventually, with the guide's help, they managed to evict it from the boat.

"I think that seal needs a bath," someone said.

"They pick up those odors from the algae that are in the water," the guide said.

The rest of the tour was uneventful. When the tour got back to the port Mark headed into the downtown area to catch a late meal. By the next morning, he was ready for his cruise.

He had arranged for a cabin on an outside wall of the cruise ship that had a large window in it. It was his first cruise and he wanted to enjoy the views as the ship travelled to its various ports. He didn't realize at the time that most people on a cruise spent their time in the day outside their cabins, and not inside their cabins. Despite this, the cabins came with a TV with satellite reception for over 100 channels, a sofa, and a study area.

One of his friends had told him that you can get lost on a cruise ship. They had advised him to put some pictures on his cabin door so that he could still recognize it if he forgot its number. He put a magnet, with a picture of a raccoon on it, above his cabin's door handle when he checked in on his first day. That picture ended up helping him to find his cabin on more than one occasion during the cruise.

During the first day on board, Mark and everyone had to take part in a safety drill. While he was participating in it, Mark noticed another cruise ship pass by that had a small submarine hanging off of the side of it. He wondered what that was all about.

He asked one of the staff, "Why does that cruise ship have a submarine?"

"Some of our cruise ships give underwater tours in the bays that we visit. It is a new addition to our cruises," the staff member informed him.

He hoped that his cruise ship had a submarine as well!

On his first three days of cruising, he explored the ship from stem to stern.

The ship had a dozen levels and was about 900 feet long. The ship had several movie theatres, restaurants, night clubs, video game rooms, computer rooms, exercise areas, spas, pools, tennis courts, lounge areas, and a shopping mall! It even had several elevators on board! He had heard about another cruise ship that even had a golf course inside it. He wondered if any of them had race tracks inside them. He never did find a submarine onboard his cruise ship.

Mark figured that he actually lost weight in the first few days that he was exploring the ship. Later, he gained it all back, from all of the excellent food that he ended up enjoying during his cruise.

Even later, he kept discovering unknown rooms and areas at the ends of long corridors that he had originally thought were just for servicing the rooms on each side of them. He wasn't sure if he should have *discovered* some of those rooms, since they had all kinds of machinery in them. He even discovered where the captain and the crew were hiding out in the evening.

He also managed to attend several events during the cruise that were scheduled in the movie theatres. There were the regular movies, but also concerts, plays, magic shows, ballets, and operas. On top of these, there were fireworks every night. He joined the other passengers on the upper decks to enjoy these bright pyrotechnical light shows.

At the end of the first week of the cruise, he departed the ship at one of their ports of call in order to take in a full day ride on a historic steam train. For reasons that he was soon to discover for himself, most of his fellow passengers avoided the train in favor of a day spent shopping in the port.

That train had wound its way through narrow gorges, past roaring rapids, over shaking bridges, and up the sheer side of cliff faces. It was thrilling!

After the train trip was over, Mark joined his fellow passengers who were taking a shortcut back to the cruise ship. They had seen a trail that ran alongside a manufacturing area. It seemed to head straight back to the ship, and it was a much shorter route than going around the huge yard that the manufacturers were located in. All was going well until the trail ended at a sharp drop off into the sea. There was a fence that extended a few feet beyond the land. They couldn't just go around it.

"End of the trail," someone said.

Most of them just shrugged their shoulders and then backtracked so that they could take the correct route back to their ship. One of their members decided to climb up and around the fence while hanging perilously over the drop to the sea.

Mark shouted to him, "Come back with us. The time that you'll save is not worth the risk of injury to yourself."

The last that they saw of him, he had made it to the other side and he was striding confidently through the manufacturing area. They never did see him on the ship again. Some people joked that the dogs in the manufacturing yard must have got to him. Either that or the constables in the area must have picked him up for trespassing.

By the second week, Mark had started to unwind and to just relax on the upper decks of the ship. He began to reflect back upon his life, and upon the things that he had seen in his studies, in his work, and in his academic classes while he was teaching them.

'There is so much that I could share with students and with others,' he thought.

He had often thought during his studies that there must be a better way to conduct courses and he had tried to do this in his own classrooms. During his years of working, he often wondered why the universities did not teach everything that he was learning.

Making up his mind to do something about the situation, he sought out the purser to get some writing pads and pens. Over the next few days as he sat looking out over the calming ocean, he put down his thoughts on paper.

First, he focused on the systems that he had built for electronic commerce for businesses, the classes that he had taught concerning it and the doctoral courses that he himself had taken on the subject. He wrote down a few areas regarding some of the concepts for it that all businesses should understand. He examined the impact that electronic commerce had on the various departments in a business, the ways to improve marketing with it, and the trends that he had observed happening with it.

As he was writing down his thoughts on this, he considered the financial systems that he had seen, designed or built for businesses. He wondered if he could come up with some basic designs that he could share with technical people who had to support such systems. He had taken graduate courses concerning these systems, and he had taught a number of business and computer courses for them as well. It took him a while longer to sketch out a framework of what was needed.

Finally, he turned his attention to all of the MBA courses that he had taught. A lot of material was covered in them but he had only observed a few key components during his two decades of consulting that were extensively used by businesses. He wanted to create some kind of manual, or book, which could be used by business people to analyze and improve their operations. He would start with a description of how to assess the overall economic and marketing environments, and then move onto the methods that could be used to analyze business operations.

When he was finished, he was surprised to learn that the cruise was already coming to an end. When he got back home, he would have to expand on the notes that he had started this trip and then contact some publishers. He still had to make up some notes for a new course that he had been given to teach next term.

Mark thought back on the many journeys that he had made in previous years, and he hoped for many new journeys in the years to come.

Chapter 16: Travels

An ant on the move does more than a dozing ox. (Lao Tzu)

The first major journey that Mark made early in his life was a trip to China, after his second year at university. He would be starting a part time job in the next couple of months, and he was wondering what he could do in the first part of his summer break. That was when he saw an advertisement from a large research university. They wanted to recruit students for a trip to China for a few weeks for a research study.

After tracking down sponsorship from local businesses to pay for the trip, Mark was on his way. He wasn't sure if this would be like a camping trip or just a trip to a few new cities. So he packed everything that he could think of.

His father had frequently taken him on camping trips during his teenage years. He had been taught to be prepared for anything. He had learned how to build a campsite, and how to live off of the land, the rivers, and the lakes.

When he arrived in China, the customs people were very interested in some of the items that were in his luggage. "What are these for?" they asked him.

"That is to start fires for cooking. That is for pounding in wooden stakes to put up temporary housing. And those are for cooking any fish or animals that I find."

They laughed at him, and then called their buddies over to see what he had brought into their country.

"We are quite civilized here in China. You will not need any of this. We suggest that you just leave it in storage here at the airport, and then get a small backpack to carry your personal goods around with you."

Mark followed their advice but he could not believe how cheap everything was in China. He bought a large backpack and then loaded it up with items that he found for sale. He was surprised when he saw some of the vendors at the airport using an ancient abacus to calculate the total of his items. The other students, who had come along for the trip, including the administrator from the university, were also loading up on souvenirs. They already had large backpacks with them. Mark figured that they had travelled a lot more than he had.

The government had arranged for tour guides and various officials to accompany the students on their travels around China. There were two dozen students in their group. A small bus and driver was also assigned to them.

The first order of business was to drive all of them over to a hotel to get them settled in. They would only be staying a few days before they would be taken to other cities. Since those cities were spread throughout China, everyone would be taking either planes or trains to them.

As they were driven through the streets, Mark could not help but notice how many bicycles were sharing the roads with cars, and how many people were walking in the roads as well. He tried to figure out their traffic rules but he finally gave up. They seemed to just go wherever and whenever they wanted. The honking, tire screeching, and shouting was unbelievable. It was amazing that there were no accidents!

The next morning, they were taken to see an assortment of schools, factories, and hospitals. Mark noticed that the hospitals were using both traditional herbal medicines as well as western medical practices. He kept notes on everything that their guides were saying and on all that he saw. He was able to obtain several contacts from the factories that he could pass on later to those businesses that had sponsored him.

In the next few days, his group also visited more factories, some classes at a local university, and a military base. He had never seen so many tanks, helicopters, fighter jets, and soldiers in his life. It looked like there was a major practice exercise going on. His group's use of cameras was closely monitored during that time.

By the end of the week, they were all shuffled off to a train station for a journey to the next city. The clickety-clack of the train on the rails gave Mark a constant headache. While he was walking down the aisle in the train to go to the next car, he met another student coming from the other direction. The aisles were so narrow that he could not pass by him!

"Would you like to hang out the window so that I can pass you, or should I do it?"

"Why don't we just ask the people in the cabin beside us if they'd mind opening their door, so that one of us can squeeze into it for a moment? I've been doing that for the last hour."

That sounded like an excellent idea to Mark. He was learning new customs during all of the time that he was spending in China. He had already learned the proper etiquette for entering rooms and for eating. There were so many rules to remember that he would have to start making up a guide book pretty soon.

At other cities, he added to his knowledge of China's manufacturing systems, and of their educational systems.

He liked what he was seeing for practical education. The students in China would learn concepts in the morning, and then they would apply those concepts in the afternoon at nearby cooperating businesses and factories.

Mark wished that his university training was just as focused on practical matters. He hoped that one day he could encourage all universities to do similar things. Even just a few field trips per term to businesses and factories would be beneficial for understanding the practical side of course materials.

On one day, the group that Mark was with was taken on a short river cruise for a few hours to the next city. They were the only group on that small passenger ship. It was a peaceful trip, and Mark spent most of it gazing out over the side of the ship at the passing countryside. The sweet aroma of fresh blooms from the bushes along the sides of the shore greeted him at every turn of the river.

He was amazed at the number of splendid temples that he saw in the surrounding hillsides. Some of them looked like they had been built hundreds of years ago. All of them appeared to be well preserved.

When their group finally arrived at the other city, they were taken to the Chinese version of an opera show. Mark thought that it would be boring, but the show was filled with lots of colorful costumes and martial arts movements.

On the final day of their trip he was nominated by his fellow students to give a speech to thank their hosts. He spent most of the day trying to compose something suitable to say. When he gave his speech at the end of the day it was translated by an interpreter and it was received with great applause. He always wondered if they had translated what he had said, or if they had said something else that was more eloquent.

That trip was a cultural awakening for him plus it forever changed his way of thinking about education.

The research university had also arranged for all of the students to visit Japan for a few days, before they headed back to their own country. They even got to take high speed trains to several cities in Japan. Mark could not believe how crammed with people the trains were. He would never complain about city transit back home again!

In one of the cities, they were taken to a Sumo wrestling match.

"Look at that!" someone shouted.

Mark could see a couple of big wrestlers that appeared to weigh several hundred pounds each. They were pushing each other around a ring. He tried to figure out the rules but all that he could determine was that you had to push your opponent out of the big circle in the ring, or to trip your opponent down to the ground.

In other cities, they were often taken to well-manicured gardens. They were breath taking in their beauty and elegance. In one of them, Mark saw a stunningly beautiful Geisha lady pass by. He wondered if he could persuade her to come back to his country for his graduation, in order to be his wife for a graduation present.

He was amazed by all of the industrialization that he had seen during his trip. After he got back, he was always thinking about how he could apply the concepts in his classes to various business situations. He wanted to learn as much as he could about business processes and technology.

It seemed to him that there was so little time during his undergraduate years at the university to study all of the required material that was needed for a good job.

Once he graduated, he did not do any other major traveling for the next few years except for his business trips to other cities. For sure, those trips were nice but most of them were not exceptional. However, he still got to see a variety of businesses, as well as parts of the country, that he was not even aware of.

Some of the scenery, events, museums, and architectural styles that he saw were truly awe inspiring!

He had stood on the lips of canyons and walked along the edges of scenic canals. He had also observed incredible air shows, seen battle re-enactment plays that were conducted in vibrant period costumes on rolling hills, and had watched a number of horse jumping competitions. Plus the museums in all of the cities contained a rich heritage of artifacts for everyone to discover.

He was able to enjoy art museums, ancient armory museums, and a variety of other aircraft and military museums.

The next major trips occurred for him when he joined an international consulting company, which then sent him to countries around the world. Most of the countries that he was sent to were in the Far East since a lot of manufacturing activities occurred in those areas. He always tried to arrange for two or three days at the end of his trips, in order to investigate their local cultures.

He recalled one memorable trip when he had been sent to Malaysia for two weeks.

The business client made an effort to bring him to historic sites at the end of each day. Many of them had stone forts that were still standing and some had working cannons. Mark was tempted to fire off one of the cannons when no one was looking.

The client also personally escorted him on weekends to the local markets, and to the other sites around the city. He met several other business families during those trips. He was able to bring back many new clients for his consulting company.

This was also the first time that he saw an elephant. One of the sites that the client brought him to on the weekend had some elephants on display. Tourists were given food to give to the elephants, in order to get to know the elephants better. Mark decided to have some fun with an elephant, and so he hid the food behind his back. The next thing that he knew, the elephant was poking him in his stomach with its trunk.

"Hey!"

He relented and then gave the food to the elephant. He had heard that elephants remember forever. He hoped that he did not meet that elephant on his next trip to Malaysia.

There was a show right after that. The elephants were dressed in scary war costumes, and their handlers showed how they could be used in battles to vanquish enemies. Now Mark really hoped that the elephant did not remember him!

As the trip was ending, the client asked him, "What will you do for the next couple of days before you fly back to your own country?"

"I always just wander around to see what I can discover."

"That won't do. There is so much more that you could see at the nearby city. Let me make some calls and see if I can arrange the details for you."

Mark was surprised when the client came back to him a few hours later. The client arranged for a driver to take him to the next city. He also arranged for a hotel for a couple of days, and for a tour guide to accompany Mark to show him around the city.

"That sounds great. Let me know how much all of this will cost and then I will pay you with some of my traveler's checks."

"Don't even think about it. I appreciate all of the help that you have given to my business. It is my pleasure to return the favor."

There were similar favors granted to Mark over the years. He never got around to planning his own vacations until he started teaching for a university. His business trips gave him ideas about the kinds of places that he would like to visit, and the kinds of things that he would like to see.

He was not even sure if there were any more interesting places in the world left to visit after his many business trips to cities in various countries. He had not done much travel in Europe but he knew that he definitely wanted to see some of the castles that they had. He had not done any travel to islands, or on cruises, and so he wanted to check out those as well.

Trips to countries in Europe were easy to plan. He booked a tour to one of them one summer and spent a few days exploring every castle that he could find. And some of them were really hard to find! He thought back to his university days when he had first learned fencing and he had felt like a pirate. Now he felt like a knight from ancient times and he tried to imagine what lives were like back then. The pageantry in their courtyards must have been glorious!

While he was touring around the area, he was also able to see several majestic cathedrals and palaces. He even visited some historic estates that had impressive mansions on them, and he was able to take in a number of the colorful festivals in the nearby villages and towns.

That same summer, he rented a recreational vehicle to travel around his own country. The vehicle was the size of a small bus and it had all of the comforts of a home inside it. Behind the driver's area were a couple of large swivel chairs and a sofa for relaxing on. Next to them were a dining area on one side and a fully stocked kitchen on the other side. Towards the rear of the vehicle was a complete washroom and an enclosed bedroom with a king sized bed in it.

Mark had not spent much time exploring the countryside in recent years, and all that it had to offer. There were national parks to visit, lakes to see, glaciers to see, and mountainous areas to explore. He saw lots of wildlife but fortunately he did not meet any bears while he was hiking around the various areas that he visited. He even discovered some natural hot springs in the mountains near an old abandoned mining town. He was worried about ghosts and so he did not linger long at that location.

Later in his trip he dropped in on some apple and strawberry farms. Customers were allowed to pick as much as they wanted to. They were supposed to put everything into baskets that were weighed when they checked out. Mark had to admit that he probably put one strawberry into his mouth for every few that he put into the basket that he was carrying. Those were his actions, at least at the beginning. That is until he got full.

It was a glorious summer, and it helped to relax him. It opened his mind to the other pleasures that life had to offer instead of just spending all of his time studying various topics.

He realized that once he had put in all of the hard work to get to a good position in life then he could start enjoying it.

The next year, he booked a trip to a small island in the middle of an ocean. He had never seen so much water in all his life! And he didn't even know how to swim!

The first thing that he did upon reaching the island was to find a tour that went out on a sailboat to look at ocean life. He was delighted by the dolphins that followed the sailboat out, and by his sightings of whales throughout the trip. A stiff breeze came in that rustled the sails, and then the seas started to get rougher as the day wore on.

When the boat started to toss around in the waves, Mark scrambled to the very front of the sailboat, in order to more fully appreciate the ocean spray. He loved the sea!

The next day, he rented a powered hang glider to fly around the island. It looked like a go-kart with a propeller behind it, with a huge hang glider above it. It was controlled with a central bar, just like a hang glider. Once he had the motor started, then he pushed out on the bar to take off. When he slid the bar to the left, or right, it allowed him to steer the ultralight aircraft. He could simply pull the bar towards himself whenever he wanted to descend. His other option was to just turn off the motor to gracefully descend to a smooth landing.

He had a great couple of hours skimming along the coasts of the island, as well as flying over its many river valleys.

The following day, he managed to find a pilot that could take him up in a sailplane high above the island. When the other pilot found out that he also flew airplanes, he let him take the controls to check out the aircraft. By circling around, Mark had a panoramic view of the island below him, of its glistening white beaches, and of the crystal blue waters that surrounded it. It was exhilarating!

There was absolute silence in the sailplane. Mark felt that he was truly flying and at one with the majestic clouds around him.

Later in the week, he approached a local university that was doing marine research in the area. He informed them that he was a university professor and then he spent some time discussing their research, as well as his own research.

"Would you like to come down with us tomorrow, Mark? We have our own small research submarine."

Mark was speechless for a moment. "Of course I would. I would love to get a closer look at the ocean life under the sea, and at the beautiful coral reefs that are around here."

The following day was enchanting, and the memories of it have always been foremost in his mind. He had the opportunity in later years to go down in some tourist submarines but it was not the same type of experience.

He also visited some naval museums where they had some older submarines that you could walk through. He could not believe how cramped the living conditions were in the real submarines. At a much earlier point in his life he had even considered serving in them. He was fascinated by naval technology.

On that trip, Mark had enjoyed time on the water, under the water, and over the water.

There were many more trips to islands in the ensuing years. He never grew tired of them and sometimes he thought about transferring to a university on one of them. It would have been great to have conducted classes in a university during the day, and then to have gone out onto the ocean later in the afternoon.

One of his more adventuresome trips occurred during a time in Mexico. He booked a boat tour that also included a horse ride into the jungles of Mexico. He had ridden horses early in his life when he used to help out his uncles, and so he enjoyed being with the horses. And they seemed to enjoy being with him.

The boat trip was picturesque with many stops in various coves along the way, before getting to the drop off point for the jungle trip.

After everyone on the trip had mounted the horses, the guide took them through a path in the jungle past a few local villages. Mark found it interesting to see what true jungle life was like as he looked around. There was a well in the center of the villages and some of them had a small marketplace off to one side of it. The houses looked like something right out of a movie. It was so peaceful there.

Then the real adventure started!

The guide came up to a wide river and he expected everyone to cross it to continue the trip on the other side. Half of the group turned back on the spot. This seemed to be too much of an adventure for them.

Little did Mark and the others know what was still to come!

As Mark was encouraging his horse to cross the river, he got into some very deep parts in it, and he had to climb on top of his horse's saddle to keep from getting wet. He thought, '*I should have brought a bathing suit.*'

There was some additional travel through narrow jungle paths but no more villages were seen. At one point, a flock of multicolored birds startled him and his horse.

Another river was reached where the guide asked everyone to dismount from their horses. He asked them to roll up their pants and to follow him across the river. Mark now knew that he should definitely have brought a bathing suit. The group lost a few more members who decided to just stay with the horses until everyone else came back.

A couple of people lost their balance crossing the river and got thoroughly soaked, but Mark managed to keep his balance. By this time in the trip, he was so drenched in sweat from the sweltering heat that he almost decided to join them by just jumping in to cool off. But he was glad that he decided to wait to see what else was in store for their group.

On the other side of the river around a bend in the trail, a magnificent roaring waterfall suddenly came into view. Its spray was quite cooling, and it was very much appreciated by everyone. At the foot of it was a small local restaurant, along with some refreshments for their group. Mark had never had to work so hard for a meal in his life!

On the way back, his horse suddenly veered off the trail and trotted down into an extremely narrow rock strewn canyon.

The guide shouted after him, "Don't worry. That horse has a mind of his own and he knows the area quite well. He will bring you back to the big river using a route that he likes."

Mark could think of a few words that he would like to shout back at the guide, and at the horse for that matter. On the positive side, he did get to see parts of the jungle that none of the others saw. He even caught a glimpse of an animal watching him from a remote hilltop that could have been a jaguar. He hoped that his horse was good at galloping.

A few days later, he visited a local zoo in Mexico. The zoo people allowed him to go into the cages to play with some younger lions, tigers, and jaguars. They also offered him the chance to go and play with the screaming monkeys, but after seeing how mischievous they were, he declined. Overall, it was a great trip and he obtained many pictures from it.

When he got back home, he discovered that there was a farmer, about two hours' drive away that was raising lions and tigers to sell to zoos around the world. He gave the farmer a call and asked him if he could come over to visit. The farmer also let him go into the cages to play with the younger animals.

After that, whenever Mark had some free time on the weekends he would drive out to the farmer's private zoo to *play* with the lions and tigers. He often wished that he could have a pet tiger in his own home, and then he could surprise all of his neighbors when he took it out for a walk.

This year, he had fully enjoyed his ocean cruise as well. It was well planned and he was able to reassess his life, and to get a lot accomplished during his time on that cruise.

Chapter 17: The Plan

Teachers open the door but you must walk through it yourself.
(Chinese Proverb)

Now that the university term was over and Mark was back from his cruise, he felt that he could catch up on his other activities. The work on his books was going well and so he decided to focus his efforts for a while on the courses that he taught at the university.

He needed to update the examples in his courses to keep them relevant to current business practices. The university had also given him a new course to teach next term, and he would need to plan out what was in it.

He started his preparations by reviewing publications that he had seen over the last term. Many of them gave him some great ideas on items that his students would be interested in hearing about. Next he searched for current research on the use of new technology in businesses. From this he was able to adjust his class notes, and to make up some new examples for his students.

He found that one of the new technologies was not currently being taught in any university. He felt that it could represent a major change in the way that systems were developed in the future. It made it much easier to control manufacturing processes, and it could be used to enhance security systems as well.

After a few searches, he was able to locate a local supplier who was selling the new technology to manufacturers in the city. The supplier was located in an industrial complex at the other side of the city.

Mark wondered what other technologies were being used by the local manufacturers. He would have to call some of them up later to see if he could arrange field trips for his students. That way, his students could better understand how their course materials could be applied to manage various business and technological processes.

Upon driving over to the industrial complex, he told the staff at the technology supplier, "I am doing some research for the university. Would I be able to purchase this new device that you are selling to the factories? I want to do some experimenting on it, in order to see whether we could start teaching it to the students at the university."

"That sounds like a great idea. If you can get the students excited about it then we could probably sell a lot more of them once your students start graduating and recommending them to businesses."

Mark brought his new *toy* home and spent a day trying to figure out how to interface it into his computer system. Over the next few days, he developed several programs for it to see just how useful it could be. He took material from other courses that he had already taught, and expanded on it to build a new course around the new technology.

By the time that he was finished, he was really excited about the technology, and what it could potentially do.

He wrote up a summary of the new technology, the benefits that it had, and proposed a course outline that could be used to teach it. He sent all of it off to the dean of his department and hoped for the best. With luck, he would be allowed to teach about this new technology sometime during the next year.

'*I wonder what I should put into the new course that I've just received,*' he started thinking.

The university had finally gotten budgetary approval to offer the course. However, all that they had given him was a general description of what the course was supposed to include in it.

Mark wanted to create a course that could help his students to get high paying jobs in businesses.

He began his construction of the new course by looking for relevant textbooks that he could use in it. The publishers were more than happy to send him sample copies of their books. They were hoping that he would choose their book for his course.

Mark's library at home was full of books that he had collected over the years from various publishers. Sometimes they even sent him books in the hope that he would create a course based on it. Sometimes Mark pretended that he was teaching a course, just so that he could get lots of free books on the topics in a course.

A week later, while he was in the process of reviewing the table of contents for all of the books that he had received, he was finally able to narrow down the collection of books to one that would be useful for the course. It seemed to cover most of the topics that the university wanted in the course.

Next, he read the book in detail and made up some notes as he went along. He highlighted the examples that he was seeing, and he began to think about what type of assignments that he could make up from the book's contents. From his notes, he was able to plan out the material that he wanted to teach in each week, and which chapters and pages that he would like the students to read.

He found that there were some chapters that he could not use, and a couple of relevant chapters were missing from the textbook that he had chosen. He had to do some more searching through current business articles, in order to find enough material to use for teaching the missing chapters.

He also called up the publisher to see if they offered any computer resources for students, such as abbreviated notes for the chapters, or practice tests. Mark liked to provide his students with as much help as he could give them.

"Thank you for calling Professor Klepin. This book has the same resources that you saw in one of our other books that you used a couple of years ago. Your class will really appreciate it. May we send you some more books that we have recently published on other technologies? Perhaps you could use them in your future courses as well?"

Mark just sighed. "Of course. The more the merrier," he said. '*You can run but you can't hide,*' he thought.

Upon going through the examples in the textbook, he discovered a few of them that either had miscalculations, or that were missing the steps that explained how they got their final results.

It took him another couple of days to track down better explanations from current business practices. For some of them, he just made up new material that was based on his own experiences from when he was working.

By this time, he was ready to begin making up assignments that the students could work on. He could also plan out the quizzes and exams that he would be using to test their knowledge of the material.

He wanted to make up some business situations that would allow the students to practice applying the material as they learned it. That way, they would appreciate the value of the course, and could refer back to their assignments later when they started their careers after their graduation.

He always started assignments by thinking back over the past projects that he had worked on. Then he wrote those up, and rearranged the course material so that several methods could be used to solve the problems in the assignments. This was something that he saw in his master's studies. Those programs often used real business cases to reinforce the learning of new topics.

It had been a long day. He took off the rest of it by visiting one of the popular shopping malls in his area. The mall had an atrium in the middle of it with numerous ponds, plants, and walkways. It made it seem more like a hidden paradise than a commercial building. There were several stores surrounding the atrium. He wanted to check out some of the clothing stores so that he could update his wardrobe. His students seemed to think that his dressing was too formal. He would try to surprise them in the next term with a more modern look.

He found a lot of clothing that was interesting. He couldn't wait to show it off to his students. He was holding his shopping bags and looking in a store window when a mesmerizing rose scented fragrance suddenly enveloped him. He felt someone tap him on his shoulder.

Turning around, he saw Marcia with a group of her friends behind her.

"Hi Marcia. What a pleasant surprise it is to see you again. I hope that you were satisfied with the grade that you got in my course. You were one of my better students."

"Thank you for such a nice compliment, Professor. I really enjoyed your course. I can see that you have been doing some shopping today. What else have you been up to this summer?"

"I just came back from a wonderful cruise. You should try a cruise yourself."

"I wish that someone would ask me to go on a cruise. That'd be wonderful!"

"I am sure that someone will one day. By the way, you may be interested in a new course that I will be teaching next term. You should be able to see it on the class schedules already. I have spent most of this week finalizing the notes for it. It will cover all of the latest technology that is used by businesses."

"That sounds really exciting, Professor. I'll be sure to look up the course. You're such an intriguing instructor."

Marcia then wandered off with her friends while whispering to them. Before she turned the corner into the next section of the mall, she glanced back at him and winked.

Mark was sure that students like Marcia would enjoy the new course that he was designing.

He spent another hour browsing the stores in the mall, but he could not find anything else that interested him, and so he headed home.

The next morning, he was ready to continue designing his new course.

"Time to make up the test material for this course," he said to himself.

In addition to a midterm and final exam, he wanted to have a short quiz that was given a month before each of these. These would get the students thinking about the concepts in the course. He would leave any calculations, diagrams, and the solving of sample business situations for the major exams. The quizzes would be closed book tests that would just ask for some definitions and some evaluations on the differences between methods in the course.

Once he got started, it didn't take him long to construct the quizzes from his class notes. It took him a little longer to make up the major exams for the course. On top of this, he also had to make up some alternative quizzes and exams, in case a student was unable to attend the scheduled tests.

He got up to stretch and walked over to his kitchen to brew some coffee. While he was waiting for it to brew, he gazed out of his back windows into the park that was behind his house.

He could see that several people were out today walking their dogs, or throwing Frisbees for their dogs to catch. It looked like one of the dogs had decided that it was more fun to go after the rabbits in the park instead of after the Frisbees. The rabbits were giving the dog a real workout. They seemed to be taunting him.

Mark watched this for a while but then he turned back to his kitchen to see how the coffee was coming along. There were plumes of steam coming from the pot by this time.

It wasn't long before the rich aroma of coffee filled his home. He filled a cup and sat back down to savor it, as well as to finish up the requirements for the new course.

As a final step in preparing the material for the new course, he had to assign point values to all of the assignments and tests. He also had to look at a calendar to determine the dates on which the assignments would be due, and when the tests could be conducted. He found a potential problem when he realized that one of his classes would occur on a public holiday. He had to redistribute his lecture for that day into the other lectures, in order to cover everything that was required.

Mark decided at this point that he needed to head over to the university to check out the room that they had scheduled for him for this course. He wondered if Cindy could join him over there and so he gave her a call.

"Hello?"

"Hi Cindy. This is Mark. I'm heading over to the university. They just gave me a new course to teach and I finally figured out what will be in it. I need to check out the classroom. Would you like to join me over there to discuss the course? I think that you'd like it as well."

"I can only drop by for a few minutes. I'm heading out shortly to check on some show homes. I'd like to move into a new home within a year. I'm tired of always renting and I want to have a place that I can call home."

"That sounds like a great idea! Why don't we meet over in the faculty lounge area and then I can show you what I've developed?"

Mark looked forward to seeing Cindy again. She looked outstanding, had a sharp mind and she always seemed willing to spend some time with him. He got to the university first and waited for her outside of the faculty area.

"Hi Mark. What's this new course that you are developing?"

"Come inside and sit down. I brought over the course outline and I can show it to you."

Mark opened the door for her and escorted her to the sofa by one of the windows. It was a beautiful day out and he wanted

Cindy to enjoy the sunshine. As he went to sit down beside her, the dazzle from her scintillating diamond earrings temporarily blinded him. He had never seen her looking so alluring. He spent several minutes explaining his new course to her. She seemed to be getting more excited the longer that he talked about the course.

"Isn't it a great course? I think that you could use the knowledge in it as well. It covers all of the latest technology and it shows how it's being used in businesses."

Cindy just gave him a big smile. She appeared to have other thoughts on her mind.

"Let's talk more about this at a later time."

"That would be fine. You said that you wanted to see some show homes so let me escort you to the main doors of the university."

Cindy had a slight frown on her face as he walked her out.

'She must be thinking about my course and about how she can take advantage of it,' he thought.

He decided that it was time to head over to the classroom for his new course. The university had scheduled his class in the administration building. They were running short of classrooms and so they were putting the classes wherever they could for now. He finally located the room on one of the upper floors. It looked like it had been a former meeting room for the directors of the university. The room was enormous and it had elegant wood panelling on all of its walls.

"Hey! Where are all of the computers for the students? Where is my computer for giving demonstrations? And where is the projector to show notes on the board?" he said upon entering the room.

One of the administrators was passing by and heard him. "Is there a problem, Mark?"

"Where did everything go that should be in this room?"

"I don't see a problem. The desks are there. The board is there for writing notes on."

"Those are definitely appreciated but modern educational training requires that students can practice the material as they are learning it, and the instructors can demonstrate the application of it using current software tools. Most of the other classrooms are loaded with computers and projectors."

"I'm sure that this was just an oversight. Maybe the equipment got moved to another classroom? Leave it with me. I'll have it all straightened out by the time that your course starts."

"Thanks Jim. I'd hate to think that I was being expected to go back to the Stone Age."

Jim just smirked and walked down the hallway to his office.

'*This reminds me. I still have to check out the new software for this course,*' Mark thought.

He headed home but the first thing that he did was to unwind in his sauna. He would look at the new software in the morning after he had gotten a good night's sleep.

The next day, he was ready to tackle the software for the new course.

The university had already provided a copy to him. All that he had to do was to try to figure out how to use it, and to make up some examples that he could show to his class during the next term.

He had an idea of the type of data that he wanted to use. He spent some time keying in some relevant business figures into a database that he had previously set up. He did not like to do this during a lecture since then valuable class time would be taken up by the students just watching him entering in data.

Once he had his data set up, he proceeded with loading it into the new software and experimenting with it. He tried to understand how the data could be analyzed, and the steps that were involved in doing this.

He also wanted to try out the various reports in the software, and see if they could be saved in different formats that could be sent to a manager. He was amazed at how powerful and how flexible this software appeared to be.

Finally, he looked for ways that the results of his analysis could be sent back to a database, in order that they could update the totals that would be in a data warehouse. The software performed flawlessly.

The last thing to do was to write up everything that he had done, in order to incorporate it into his notes for the new course. Mark looked forward to teaching this course next term, and he hoped that the students would enjoy the course as well.

He spent the remainder of the afternoon thinking back on his first year at a university.

Chapter 18: First Year

Quality is not an act, it is a habit. (Aristotle)

The first day that Mark Klepin had arrived at his undergraduate university had been overwhelming for him. Even though he had visited it a few times during his high school days, he still felt lost.

His parents had dropped him off but now he was on his own. His first priority was to head over to the university housing office to get settled in. He had already told them that he wanted a room for himself so that he could just focus on his studies.

The housing office had separate buildings on the campus for the guys, and other buildings for the ladies. Each building had a laundry room in the basement. The room that the housing office had assigned to him was quite small when he checked into it. The washrooms were at the end of a long hallway, and they were shared by everyone on the floor that he was on.

In other words, it was just like the home that he'd grown up in.

The staff at the housing office asked him, "Do you want to prepay for all of your meals on a term pass, or do you just want to pay for them as you go along?"

"Which is the cheaper option?" he inquired.

"The total costs for a meal pass will be significantly lower than the total cost of the individual prices for each meal. The only catch is that you'll have to eat the standard meals that we'll prepare for you."

Mark signed up for the meal pass. The university had a large cafeteria, just like a school, where the students could show up for the standard meals that were handed out to them. The meals were at fixed times each day, and the food was just basic items.

Breakfast was from 7 to 8 AM and consisted of eggs, bacon, sausage, hash brown potatoes, muffins, toast, cereal, and a variety of juices, milk, coffee, and teas. Lunch was from 12 to 1 PM and consisted of various meat dishes, vegetables, buns, potatoes, fruits, and an assortment of desserts such as pies, puddings, and ice cream. Supper was from 5 to 6 PM and it served the same meals that were served at lunch time. Mark suspected that it was just whatever was left over from lunch, but he was happy with the food selections.

The housing office also told him that if he wanted anything else then he would have to pay for individual meals at the private vendor booths that were spread around the campus. The vendor booths had choices for pizza, hamburgers, hot dogs, French fries, sushi, and a variety of dishes from many other cultures. There were also snack machines around the campus where the students could obtain chips, cookies, chocolate bars, candies, and soft drinks. But all of those cost money, and Mark did not have any extra money to spend.

His next priority was to head over to the registrar's office so that he could enroll in the courses that he would like to take in his first year. He had decided over the summer which business and computer courses that he would like to take, and he had already obtained the books for them.

He was pleasantly surprised when the university registrar offered him the chance to challenge the final exams for the courses due to his summer studies, and to jump to the second year for those courses.

He had already planned out his entire four years of undergraduate studies.

He did not want to take easy courses or fun courses. They would not be useful in his working life later on.

He only wanted to take courses that he felt could help him out with his chosen career.

Once his housing and registration was settled, Mark decided that he would just roam around the campus to see what was inside the various buildings. He also wanted to determine where all of his classes were so that he would not be wasting time trying to find them in the next week when all of the classes began.

His first stop was at the library to get familiar with their various sections. When he eventually left, he noticed that they were rolling out several trolleys of books into the hallways.

"What are those for?" he asked.

"Those are books that are being replaced. We do this at the start of each term. Anyone may take the books. If there are any books that are still on the trolleys by next week then we just throw them away."

Upon hearing this, Mark immediately began to load himself up with a number of books on various business and computer topics. He also found some books on general topics that interested him. He eventually had to ask the librarian if he could borrow another trolley so that he could wheel all of the books that he had taken back to his room.

This was a good start to his new term at the university, but there was more to come.

As he wandered around the buildings on campus, he discovered that many professors were also throwing out books at this time. They had set up tables outside of their offices with the books on them. Some of the books were even new! Mark found many that were useful, and he made several more trips back to his room.

Towards the end of the day, he discovered that the book store at the university was also having a massive sale on a number of their books. He was able to pick up quite a few for minimal costs.

By this time, there were so many books on the floor of his room that it was hard for him to move around inside it. He decided that he needed a few book cases along one wall of his room, in order to organize the collection of books that he had obtained.

That evening, he visited an office supply store which was nearby to the university, which was familiar with student needs. The store carried book cases, desks, chairs, shelving, lamps, and a variety of office stationary and other equipment. His room already had a small study desk, a lamp, and a chair. Therefore, he arranged for them to just deliver some book cases to his room in the morning.

He spent the next day organizing the books which he had collected onto the book cases. By the time that he was done, he had his own private library. When he started browsing the books, he discovered many new business and computer topics that he had not even been aware of.

He realized that he would have a lot to learn over the next few years, in addition to his regular university studies.

By the next week, he was raring to go.

He prepared a separate study binder for each of his classes to put his notes into.

Another student had told him on the weekend that the lockers around the campus were first come, first serve. So he had seized a locker that was reasonably close to most of his classes so that he could put his course textbooks into it. That would save him the trouble of running back to his room between each class to pick up the appropriate textbook, or of having to carry all of them around with him to each class.

Over the weekend he had also done laundry for the first time in his life. He put all of his clothing and towels in one of the washing machines in his dormitory and turned it on. His mother had never told him that you have to separate out colored clothing. When he opened the machine, all of his underwear and towels had turned red. He decided that he would have to replace his underwear but he liked the cool shade that his shirts had developed and so he kept them.

In his first class on Monday, he noticed that the professor spent most of the class going over the course outline, and what was expected of the students. The professor then followed this up with a short lecture on some of the basic concepts for the course, and then he assigned some relevant reading for the students to do.

After that class, Mark headed outside to head over to the building that had his next class in it. He noticed something unusual. Most of the campus was deserted.

"Where did all of the other students go?" he asked a fellow classmate, who was passing by.

"Didn't you know about all of the tunnels that are underneath this university?"

"I've never heard about them. How do you get into them?"

"You need to look for the maintenance doors inside each building. When you open them, then you'll see stairs leading down. The tunnels are not labeled, but you'll be able to figure them out fairly quickly. They are the fastest way to get between the buildings. Plus they'll allow you to avoid all of the weather that is outside."

Mark would never have thought to open up a maintenance door. He thought that they were all locked, and that they only led to rooms that were full of service equipment. In fact, he had wondered why the university had so many student janitors when he saw some of them entering one of the maintenance doors earlier that morning.

He would have to do some exploring at the end of the day. It would be like starring in an adventure movie!

While he was standing beside the other student, a sheep dashed past him. This was followed a few moments later by several students in white lab coats who were desperately trying to catch the sheep.

"What in the world?" he expressed in surprise.

"That is probably just an escapee from the veterinarian school on the campus. You would run too if you saw what they wanted to stick in you."

Mark debated whether he should join in the chase. He was quite good at catching sheep on his uncles' farms. He would have to watch out for chickens and other animals running around the campus.

Since there didn't appear to be any more excitement, he continued to head over to his next class.

His second class of the morning was much like his first class. The course outline was reviewed, and some basic concepts were presented. When the class finished, he headed over to the cafeteria to get his lunch. He had already visited it that morning for breakfast. He had also visited it a few other times over the weekend for his other meals.

While he was eating he noticed that a few of the students were going back for seconds. He turned to the students sitting at the next table, and asked them, "Excuse me. Are we allowed to go back many times for meal items?"

"Shhh! Not so loud. Officially, we're not allowed to go back for seconds. But there are so many students with meal passes that they only look at your photo on it, in order to confirm that you're allowed to collect food from them. They don't often remember whether a student has gone through their serving lines before."

Mark said, "Aha," and then snuck back to get another helping of the mouth-watering dessert for that day. He couldn't help thinking of a book that he had read, in which a little boy had asked a server, "Please, sir, I want some more."

His classes in the afternoon had gone much the same as his morning classes. He figured that the real lectures would start later in the week. He still had a lot of assigned reading to do that night, but first he wanted to explore the tunnels under the university.

He found it a challenge to find all of the maintenance doors that led to the tunnels. He should have just paid more attention during the day to where all of the students were heading to.

Once he was in the tunnels, he managed to get thoroughly lost in them. He had to constantly come out of them, in order to get his bearings, before going back down into them to explore some more. A musty smell permeated all of the tunnels. Eventually he had them all figured out. Or so he thought. His dreams that night were filled with mazes.

During the rest of the week, and in the following weeks, he found it quite useful to rewrite all of his class notes at the end of each day. This allowed him to better understand the topics, and it allowed him to organize them for easier referencing. He also started several new binders for the notes that he was making from all of the books that he had collected.

His knowledge of business and computer topics was starting to grow at a phenomenal rate. But he still had a lot more to learn!

He often maximized the number of books that he could sign out from the library at once. He tended to spend his nights surrounded by a sea of books in his room.

He figured that you only went to university once and you only took courses once, and so he wanted to make the most of his time in his studies. He felt that it was better to spend the time now to learn everything, in order to prepare for a successful career, than to struggle later trying to grasp the concepts that would be needed to do a job, or even to get a job.

Mark wondered if he would ever be standing at the front of a classroom himself one day trying to pass on a wealth of knowledge to other students, and then encouraging them to be the best that they could be in their own field of studies.

Chapter 19: The Beginning

The journey of a thousand miles begins with one step. (Lao Tzu)

As Mark awoke to the buzzer on his alarm, he realized that this was the first day of classes for a new term. He lay in his bed for a while thinking about how he would like to organize the day. He remembered how nervous he was on the first day of his classes when he was a student. After a few more minutes he jumped out of bed to get prepared for his day.

He laid out some of the *cool* clothes that he had bought over the summer. He hoped that they would impress his students. He always used to wear two or three piece suits when he taught all of his classes. However, several of his students from last term had convinced him that it was OK to relax and to just dress more casually.

Before leaving his home, he used several boxes to gather up a number of the books that he had received from various publishers. He had not opened them, and he would not be using them, but he thought that perhaps some of his students would probably appreciate them.

When he got to his office at the university, he located a small table. He put the table outside of his office with all of his extra books piled up on it. He added a sign on which he wrote 'Free books for students.' He hoped that the other faculty would get the hint. He knew that some of them would probably sneak a book or two anyways before the students could get to them.

Glancing up, he saw the dean ahead of him in the hallway. He promptly said, "Good morning, Dr. Richards."

Upon turning around, the dean replied, "Mark! I almost didn't recognize you. You are looking quite sharp today."

"My students suggested that I try a new look. By the way, what do you think of that new course proposal that I sent over to you?"

"I passed it on to the budgetary committee and I just heard that it is a go already. I will talk to you more once we schedule it in for next term. However, I will see you later this morning in your class. I am going to drop in on a few classes this week to see how the new term is going."

"It is always a pleasure to have a dean in my classes as a student," Mark said, with tongue in cheek.

He headed over to the library since he still had time before his first class started for the day. He wanted to check out what new books they had so that he could tell his students about them. He always liked to offer other books to his students that could be read besides just the official textbook. Over the summer, he had discovered several relevant books for his courses. He suggested to the librarian that she should add these to her collection of books this term as well.

It was now time for him to head over to his first class for this new term. He always liked to arrive a few minutes early before his lecture so that he could get the computers and projectors set up. He also liked to quickly review his lecture notes before each class.

He arrived to a room full of students. They all looked, well, he was not sure how they looked. Some of them were sitting quietly, staring straight ahead. A few of them saw him enter, and then they looked at him eagerly. Most of them were in groups with their friends, chatting away while glancing around at the other students.

Mark spent a few minutes getting prepared, and then he checked over the class registration list.

"Good morning! I am Professor Mark Klepin," he greeted the students.

"Good morning, sir," they said, as they scrambled into their seats.

About that time, the dean also walked in and seated himself at the back of the room. Mark nodded to him, and then continued with his lecture.

"Welcome to the course. I have taught this course a few times. Everyone always says that it is a great course, and I hope that you will also find that it is."

"Do we have to buy the textbook?" asked a student.

Seeing the dean looking at him, Mark was careful to reply, "It is the official book for this course. I will also be giving you a lot of notes, and have discussions in the class to show you how to apply the course material to actual business situations." He could see that the dean was nodding his head at the back of the room.

"Are there any other books that we can look at?" another student asked.

"It is interesting that you should bring that up. I have just been over to the library, and I gave the librarian a list of the books that are relevant for this course. Just see her and she will point out the books to you.

"Also, I have set out a number of books on various topics outside of my office door. After class, you may want to go over there as well, and to pick some up. They are free but it is first come first serve."

Mark saw a couple of students sneak out a side door. They were either rushing off to pick up the good books first, or using this opportunity to skip class. He hoped that he would see them again shortly since this was a three hour lecture.

"You may have noticed the cameras that are in the corners of the room. This is the first term our university is televising some of its lectures to another university. They have formed an academic partnership to share some of their courses."

He could that see that some of his students were giving gestures to their fellow students at the remote location. He noticed that the dean was raising his eyebrows, and rolling his eyes up at the ceiling.

"In this first lecture, I will be going over the course outline with you. I will also cover some academic issues. There will still be a short lecture at the end. The main lectures will start later in the week for this course."

"Please define short," a student asked.

"It will be about an hour and I would suggest that everyone stay for it since it will introduce the main concepts in this course. This is a three hour class, and most of the material in the lectures will show up later in your tests. However, I do give breaks every hour."

Cheering could be heard throughout the room.

"Let me start out by asking each student to call out their name and their major. I like to get to know everyone, and I also try to adjust my notes to fit in with all of the majors that you are studying. Let's do this by rows so that everyone is not shouting at once."

A few minutes later, Mark was starting to get an idea of the interests of each of his students, and he had also managed, by this time, to even remember a few of their names.

He spent the next hour reviewing the course outline. He started by explaining how the course material could be used by students in jobs when they graduated. Then he pointed out the certifications that it would allow them to get.

After that introduction, he proceeded with a discussion of the topics that would be taught each week, when the assignments were due, late policies for them, when the tests would be, and the points that would be given for each of these.

He also covered the policies on attendance, as well as other relevant university policies. He concluded by mentioning related courses that the students could take, once they had completed his course.

Since he had gone slightly past the break time that he had promised them, Mark announced that they could take a few minutes now to gather their thoughts.

The dean approached him during the break, and said, "Great presentation Mark! I won't be staying for the remainder of your lecture. I need to catch up on some work in my office, and then I will drop in on a few of the other classes today."

They shook hands, and Mark turned to chat with some of the students that had come over to see him. He noticed that the two students who had left earlier were now back in the classroom loaded with books. He hoped that they had left some books for the other students.

"Excuse me. While everyone is up and about, we will now form the groups for the group project that is in this course. Last term, I did that after the midterm but I think that it would be better if the groups could start working together earlier in the term. I need five members per group. Give me a list of the members in your groups once you have formed them."

He gave them a few more minutes to work out their group memberships, as well as to chat amongst themselves. It looked like everyone had found a group to be in for this term. Once he had the group lists in his hands, he announced, "Please take your seats. There are a few more things that I would like to make you aware of before the lecture begins."

He turned to the board and wrote the names of some business associations in a vertical list. Beside it, he wrote the names of some technical associations.

"I would like to suggest to everyone that they sign up for memberships in as many of these associations as they can. Many of them have free memberships for students, or discounted memberships for them. All of them have monthly publications, and a few of them have monthly dinner meetings, in addition to their annual gatherings.

"They are a great way to find out about new technologies, as well as current business practices. They often post jobs in their publications, and they have computer resources that you can use to locate the companies that are in their associations. Plus their meetings are a great opportunity to meet the executives in local companies."

He also wrote down the names of several prominent business and computer publications on the board.

"You may also want to consider subscribing to many of these publications. They spend their time finding and presenting current technologies and business processes to their readers so that you don't have to spend the time yourself searching for the current topics of interest."

He could see that all of the students were paying attention in his classroom now.

"This is great, sir," commented one student.

"I would further suggest that you form a study group for this class. It could meet after the class in any of the rooms that the university provides for meetings. You could use it to review the day's material. Perhaps some of you could help out your fellow classmates, and others could give mini-lectures, summarizing the material from my lectures."

Some of the students had bright eyes and were nodding their heads.

"I have also received funding from the university to form a club for this course. It will meet once a week on Fridays. We don't have labs anymore, and so I will use that club to give you extra help on the course material.

"I will give some short lectures in the club, and I have arranged for company professionals to give guest lectures in the club. Some of those companies have agreed to let me bring you to their businesses on field trips as well, in order that you can see how their operations work."

There were excited whispers among the students. Several hands went up.

Mark had to spend awhile answering all of their questions. More hands went up.

"I tell you what. Let's take our break now before the lecture starts. You can come to the front during that time to discuss the course, and these opportunities."

A crowd of students quickly gathered around Mark. They were quite excited by what the course could offer them, and they wanted to know more about his background, the kinds of projects that he had worked on, and his connections with businesses.

The break lasted for a long time before he could get the students reseated. He spent the remainder of the hour introducing basic concepts for the course, and then he bid the students on their way as they headed out for their other classes.

After lunch with the other faculty to discuss the new term, he headed over to the room for the new course that he had been given to teach.

Mark had an incredible feeling of confidence within himself as he entered the classroom that had been assigned for his business and technology course. The lecture room was packed. The course seemed to be very popular. Every seat was taken by the students. He was happy to see that computers had been installed on all of the desks, and also at the front of the room.

Some of the students recognized him as he came in. They had taken courses with him in previous terms.

"Who are you, and what did you do with our professor?" they joked with him. They had noticed his new clothing.

Mark just smiled and then walked to the lecture podium at the front of the class.

He reflected on how his students and others had changed his life for the better. He had learned that there were no true barriers in life except for those that you put up yourself. He was given limited support in his early studies and yet he had persevered with his own efforts to become successful. Even while working, he had learned that focused studies had allowed him to open up the opportunities that were available to him. Later, he had learned the value of also building up a social network with support from others to become more successful.

Even the image that he had of himself had changed. He used to be very business-like in his mannerisms and dressings but his students had helped him to relax. He had even changed his clothing and hair style to fit in with them. He wanted them to relate to him so that he could pass on his messages to them on the many ways to achieve their dreams.

As he turned around and glanced out over his current students, he could see Cindy sitting at one end of the front row, and Marcia sitting at the other end of the front row. Marcia smiled at him. Cindy smiled at him.

It was going to be another interesting term!

Reading Guide

The University Professor

The story focuses on the challenges, rewards, and setbacks, of an instructor and his students at pivotal points during a single term in a university, with flashbacks from a decade of learning, and from two decades of applying knowledge. It is autobiographical fiction, where most of the story is based on facts that occurred during the author's lifetime.

It is a light hearted look at academic life, and on how education affects all of our lives.

It starts with the instructor conducting a class and then moves on to his activities while preparing to review current material to get his students ready for their future careers. It carries through to his testing experiences and to his preparations for new courses. Every second chapter has flashbacks to those events from his past studies and work where special moments occurred that helped to mold his current character and teaching style.

Along the way, a complete study philosophy emerges.

At the start of each chapter, some words of wisdom and insight have been added from both Chinese and Western philosophers. Quotes are given by philosophers such as Lao Tzu, Confucius, Socrates, Plato, and Aristotle.

Education Discussion Questions

1. Contrast the education systems described throughout the book, with those in other countries. Consider Bachelor, Master, and PhD programs.

2. Compare PhD and DBA programs. Consult the programs at a few universities. What are their similarities? What are their differences?

3. List the methods described in the book for conducting effective classes. These can be found in the first chapter, in the last chapter, and in the review chapter. Compare them to current theories on educational training.

4. Compare the classroom experiences described in the book, for lectures and for types of test questions, to your own classroom experiences.

5. Identify ideas mentioned throughout the book that discuss the ways in which to improve the grades that are received for courses.

6. Identify current problems with education systems, and any solutions that were discussed for them in the book. What other solutions are needed?

7. Discuss the changes in education systems over the last few years that have negatively affected the quality of education. Discuss any positive changes that you have seen.

Story Discussion Questions

1. Identify the parts in each chapter that are related to the quotes at the beginning of each chapter. What lessons can be learned from them? Give examples from your own life. Discuss some of the other quotes, or sayings, that are given inside the story. What is their meaning?

2. Identify the characters in the book, their position (e.g. professor, manager, student, and so forth), and their personalities, if possible. When personalities can be determined then explain how you made your conclusions from the descriptions in the book.

3. Identify the significant turning points in the main character's life, and the subsequent decisions that were made as a result of them. Give specific examples from the book for actions that were carried out because of those decisions.

4. Describe how the main character's childhood experiences proved useful for handling the later experiences that occurred in his personal life, and in his working life. Give specific examples from the book.

5. Compare the motivations that drove the main character in his early life, to the motivations that drove him later in his professional life. What were the similarities between them?

6. Compare the high school study patterns for the main character, to his later study patterns as an adult. What events influenced his study patterns?

7. Identify all of the social interactions for the main character in the book, from both his personal life, and from his professional life. How have they shaped his personality?

8. Identify all of the countries visited in the book, along with the activities conducted in those countries. When a country is not specifically named, then discuss what country it could have been. Try to determine the actual activities that the main character could have been involved with. You may have to consult travel brochures in order to determine this.

Book Excerpt

Thank you for reading this book.

All of my books are based on my 10 years of teaching business and computer concepts in the universities, on my graduate and doctoral studies, and on my 20 years of applying concepts in industry to help businesses to become more successful.

I wish you all the best in your personal life and in your career.

Following is the complete chapter on the training of instructors from one of my previous books, which is called Life as a Professor. The book presents observations on issues that are affecting the quality of education, along with some recommended solutions that are needed to improve the value of education.

The book gives a summary of administrative issues, government issues, classroom issues, and course content issues. It also discusses changing student perceptions about education, and some new trends that are occurring in education.

* * *

All academic institutions should arrange formal training sessions for their instructors before they teach their first course. This allows the institutions to define their quality standards along with their expectations for instructors. As long as they follow through with what they are teaching the instructors then this will work well.

Most of these instructor training sessions are several weeks in length and I have been through one for each university and college that I have taught for. Unfortunately, the academic institutions do not allow you to transfer credits from previous training, like you can do with courses. I have yet to see full support for what is taught in the sessions but the institutions should practice what they preach.

The training starts with getting instructors familiar with the technology tools that the schools use to support classroom activities. The details of setting up websites for each course are covered so that notes, references, and examples can be posted for the students to assist in their learning. Chat rooms are also covered and how to properly manage discussions within them to provide useful feedback to the students. However, the websites are often considered optional and it is left up to the instructor if they will use them. Online grade books are mentioned as well (but are not made mandatory) and it is explained how they can be used to keep students up to date on their progress in a course.

Many institutions subscribe to plagiarism services that can automatically detect the parts in student papers that have been copied from others. These services look for matches on websites, on publicly available documents that can be downloaded, on electronic copies of textbooks from publishers, and on previous papers that have been submitted by students both locally and from other academic institutions. Instructors are shown how to submit student papers to these services to check for plagiarism and how to then submit reports to administration when any copied work is discovered.

Next, the institution's standards are explained to assist instructors in making up their course outlines. Topics covered include minimum assignment standards (such as word counts, APA formatting, and the use of peer-reviewed references), attendance requirements, penalties allowed for late work and plagiarism, contact information to include, and the week by week details needed for describing material to be taught. Despite this, I have still seen many course outlines approved during terms that only contain a general paragraph describing the course, a list of due dates for assessments, and the percentage that each assessment is worth.

Instructors are given the opportunity to make up sample outlines for their own courses and they are coached on how to improve them. They are shown model course outlines from previous terms as well as course outlines that are unacceptable.

Marking guidelines are discussed so that appropriate comments can be put onto papers and grading can become more of a formal process, rather than an informal one. A sample marking guideline is usually given for a typical course which states the minimum and maximum word counts, the number of references required, APA standards to be used, grammar rules, sections to be included, and the organization for papers. Point values are formally shown for excellent work versus missing work along with the allocation of points when material is only partially addressed.

Instructors are given sample papers to grade and their assessments are evaluated by the institution. During these sessions I have never seen instructors docked for marking too hard but have seen them reprimanded when they ignore the institution's standards and mark papers too lightly. However, in practice they will almost always be reprimanded for marking to standards when a student complains. Instructors are told to just take it easy and this is one of the reasons that cause education quality to start to decline.

Sample lectures are scheduled during these training sessions so that instructors can get in some practice before doing lectures in an actual classroom. Pointers are given to instructors on how to organize their lectures, how to best use their course materials, and what are some of the various teaching styles that may be used.

In one of the institutions that I taught at, the deans were allowed to pop in on any lecture at any time in order to audit the classroom environment and to verify the quality of the material that the instructor was presenting to students. I thought this was a great idea to ensure that institution standards were being followed but I have not seen this practice for many years now. I also enjoyed having the deans as students and then drilling them with questions about current practices in the workplace that the students needed to be made aware of. Maybe that is why they stopped coming around.

Typically a mentor is assigned at the end of the training sessions to guide new instructors during their first term. The mentor is someone who is familiar with the institution's standards and can assist the instructor with making up their course outline and organizing their lectures. Mentors often sit in on the lectures and provide feedback to the instructors on areas that they can improve upon. They review the course website and also any marked papers before they are handed back to the students. All institutions should use mentors and they should also reschedule mentoring sessions every year or two to help keep all instructors on track.

Other Books by the Author

All of my books are based on my 10 years of teaching business and computer concepts in the universities, on my graduate and doctoral studies, and on my 20 years of applying concepts in industry to help businesses to become more successful.

Here is a listing of my other books that you may find useful. The easiest way to find them at the various retailers is to do a search on my name, Randall Dyck, which will then pull up a current list of all of the books that I have published to date. Remember to check out my website, listed in the author section of this book, and to drop me an email sometime using the address listed on the site.

Life as a Professor

As a result of ongoing academic changes seen over the last decade, the students of today are obtaining a poorer understanding of material, which means that they are less prepared for jobs in the workplace and employers are reluctant to hire them when they graduate. Less courses are being offered in various subject areas, less details are being presented in those courses, the number of assignments is reducing, the assignments have become more brief and easier to do, less reading is required, less reference material is being given, and tests are becoming more basic.

This book presents observations about the declining quality of content delivered in courses at universities and colleges, possible reasons for these changes, as well as some recommended solutions that are needed. Follow along as the issues are presented and perhaps, together, we can make positive changes now that will protect the future and value of education.

MBA Strategic Analysis

The purpose of this book is to assist businesses in assessing their strengths so that opportunities for growth may be most effectively implemented. The material is based on my industry experience, on my graduate studies of business, and on my lecture notes for business courses that have accumulated over the last few years. It is composed of over 60 chapters and begins with an analysis of the organization and the economic and marketing environment that it operates within and then proceeds with an analysis of where it wants to be along with an examination of each component that will contribute to its goals and implementation methods to use.

E-Commerce Concepts

This book is a mix of practical and conceptual knowledge for e-commerce that discusses strategies to use when a business wants to take advantage of e-commerce to increase their sales and international exposure. The material is based on my industry experience, my doctoral studies of e-commerce, and on my lecture notes for e-commerce that have accumulated over the last few years. It is composed of over 20 chapters and is intended mainly for business people that need to understand the issues involved with e-commerce activities, and for marketers who want to learn how to take advantage of e-commerce. Technology students may also find value from it in order to understand why businesses are asking for some features. The book discusses concepts for the technologies involved, the business issues, legalities of activities, strategies which can be used, and the emerging trends.

Computerized Financial Systems

This book gives technical people an idea of how to design functional financial systems within computer database systems. The material is based on my industry experience, on my doctoral studies of computer science, and on my lecture notes for business and computer courses that have accumulated over the last few years. It covers basic financial concepts and then gives ideas on how accounting information can be recorded and processed in databases. It discusses general ledgers, receivables, payables, inventory, and fixed asset systems, as well as others. All file structures are explained, along with sample data, diagrams for the structures, and suggestions for other changes that can be done to accommodate multi-company and multi-currency situations.

About the Author

Dr Randall Dyck has taught over 5,000 students at 5 different academic institutions over the last decade. He originally spent 20 years in industry designing and building systems for retail firms, transportation firms, manufacturers, insurance firms, airlines, and oil and gas firms. He holds both PhD and MBA degrees and is certified in a number of technology and business areas.

Read more at rdyck.mynucleus.ca.

Made in the USA
Charleston, SC
30 April 2016